THREE CENTURIES OF GIRLS' EDUCATION

THREE CENTURIES OF GIRLS' EDUCATION

Regulations of the Ursuline Nuns
of the Congregation of Paris

TRANSLATED AND ANNOTATED,

WITH AN INTRODUCTION AND COMMENTARY, BY

MARY ANNE O'NEIL

LOUISIANA STATE UNIVERSITY PRESS

BATON ROUGE

Published by Louisiana State University Press
lsupress.org

DESIGNER: Andrew Shurtz
TYPEFACE: Eldorado

COVER PHOTOGRAPH:
Graduating class of 1900, Ursuline Academy, Laredo, Texas.
General Photograph Collection, Image 076-0106,
University of Texas at San Antonio Special Collections.

LIBRARY OF CONGRESS CATALOGING-IN-PUBLICATION DATA

Names: O'Neil, Mary Anne, 1945– editor, translator, author of commentary.
Title: Three centuries of girls' education : Regulations of the Ursuline nuns of the
    Congregation of Paris / translated and annotated, with an introduction and
    commentary, by Mary Anne O'Neil.
Other titles: Règlemens des Religieuses Ursulines de la Congrégation de Paris. English.
Description: Baton Rouge : Louisiana State University Press, 2022. | Includes index.
Identifiers: LCCN 2022007945 (print) | LCCN 2022007946 (ebook) | ISBN 978-0-
    8071-7788-4 (cloth) | ISBN 978-0-8071-7884-3 (paperback) | ISBN 978-0-8071-
    7869-0 (pdf) | ISBN 978-0-8071-7868-3 (epub)
Subjects: LCSH: Catholic Church—Education—France—Paris—History—Sources. |
    Girls—Education—France—Paris—History—Sources. | Christian education of
    girls—France—Paris—Sources. | Ursulines—France—Paris—History—Sources.
Classification: LCC LC506.F82 P38413 2022 (print) | LCC LC506.F82 (ebook) |
    DDC 371.8820944/361—dc23/eng/20220706
LC record available at https://lccn.loc.gov/2022007945
LC ebook record available at https://lccn.loc.gov/2022007946

To my mother,
Connie St. Romain O'Neil,
LSU Medical School
class of 1941

CONTENTS

ACKNOWLEDGMENTS ix

INTRODUCTION I

ONE
The Ursulines:
First Women Educators of France
15

TWO
A Comparison of
the 1705 and 1860 *Regulations*
51

THREE
The Ursuline Method
in the Twentieth Century
79

*Regulations of the Ursuline Nuns
of the Congregation of Paris* (1705)
93

INDEX 169

ACKNOWLEDGMENTS

I would like to acknowledge and thank Mary Lee Berner Harris, archivist of Ursuline Academy in New Orleans, and Sister Thomas More Daly, OSU, curator of the Ursuline archives in St. Louis, Missouri. Mary Lee helped me define my project by giving me access to correspondence from the first Ursulines in New Orleans and school catalogs dating back to the late nineteenth century. Sister Thomas More Daly generously researched and found several rare documents by and about Mother St. Jean Martin. Without her help I would not have been able to include this third book in my study. Yves Morin, professor emeritus of the University of Montreal's Department of Linguistics and Translation, was kind enough to share his research on early French teaching manuals and made me aware of André Chervel's *Histoire de l'enseignement du français du XVIIe au XXe siècle*, which synthesizes the complex history of French-language instruction over four centuries. I would also like to thank my longtime colleague and friend Culley Jane Carson for editing my introduction and commentary and my husband, Patrick Henry, for checking my translation for readability and accuracy.

THREE CENTURIES OF GIRLS' EDUCATION

INTRODUCTION

IN 2014, THE AMERICAN ASSOCIATION OF TEACHERS OF FRENCH
scheduled its annual summer convention in my native city of New Orleans,
Louisiana. As I searched for a subject to present at the conference, one that
went beyond the expected discussions of Cajun food, jazz, or Mardi Gras,
I hit upon the idea of talking about the elementary school I attended from
pre-kindergarten through eighth grade in the 1950s, Ursuline Academy.
Founded in 1727 by French nuns of the Order of Saint Ursula (OSU), Ursuline Academy of New Orleans is the oldest continuously operating school
for girls in the United States and, according to the school's website, the oldest
Catholic school in the United States.

I chose to talk about the Ursulines because of their importance in the
history of France and the United States as well as in the city of New Orleans.
Although the sixteenth-century founder of the Ursulines, Angela Merici, was
Italian, her company of laywomen devoted to the care and education of girls
flourished most notably as a religious order in France in the seventeenth and
eighteenth centuries. When France set up a colony in Canada in the mid-seventeenth century, Ursulines joined the missionary efforts of the Jesuits and
sailed to Quebec, where they cared for and taught Native women as well as
the daughters of colonists. In 1727, Ursulines from Rouen traveled to New

Orleans, supposedly to serve as nurses in a military hospital. True to their original mission, however, while they waited for the hospital to be built, they established a convent with both a boarding school for the daughters of French colonists and a day school for the daughters of indigenous tribes and slaves. The 1745 structure that housed the convent schools, financed in part by Louis XV, still stands in the French Quarter and is considered the oldest building in the Mississippi Valley.

The New Orleans Ursulines managed to preserve the French language and traditions of their schools despite forty years of Spanish rule, from 1763 to 1802, only to find themselves about to be swallowed up by the Protestant, English-speaking United States at the time of the Louisiana Purchase in 1803. They handled the matter by writing directly to Thomas Jefferson, asking him to guarantee their property and the right to teach. In a personal reply, Jefferson guaranteed the Ursulines "that it will be preserved to you sacred and inviolate, and that your institution will be permitted to govern itself according to its own involuntary rules, without interference from the civil authority."[1] A decade later, the general and future president Andrew Jackson credited the prayers of the Ursulines for his defeat of overwhelming numbers of British troops during the Battle of New Orleans.

My visit to the archives of Ursuline Academy in February 2014 reminded me of this history, most of which I had learned as a child but had long forgotten. I also had the chance to examine the ornate needlework done by Ursulines from Cuba during the four decades that Louisiana was a Spanish possession. I read a replica of the letter sent by President Thomas Jefferson at the time of the Louisiana Purchase as well as a copy of the letter of thanks from Andrew Jackson for the prayers that had miraculously helped him win the Battle of New Orleans in January 1815.

The archives also introduced me to a substantial library of fiction and historical studies concerning the New World Ursulines. The best known is Willa Cather's 1931 novel *Shadows on the Rock*, which takes place in eighteenth-century Quebec and portrays the nuns as surrogate mothers for the young heroine, a motherless child of French colonists. In *The Ursulines, Nuns of Adventure*,[2] the Louisiana novelist Harnett Kane transforms the French

1. Quoted by Sister Jane Frances Heaney, OSU, in *A Century of Pioneering: A History of the Ursuline Nuns in New Orleans, 1727–1827* (New Orleans: Ursuline Nuns of New Orleans, 1993), 223–24.

2. Harnett Kane, *The Ursulines, Nuns of Adventure* (New York: Vision Books, 1959).

Ursulines who traveled to New Orleans in 1727 into romantic figures. They overcome the hardships of an ocean voyage, tropical storms, and encounters with pirates as they establish their schools in the midst of malaria epidemics, military skirmishes, and changing governments. In the 1940s, an Ursuline nun and scholar, Sister Jane Frances Heaney, OSU, wrote *A Century of Pioneering: The Ursulines of New Orleans, 1727–1827*, a history of the order's first one hundred years in New Orleans. Throughout her carefully researched study, she dramatizes the frequent conflicts between the nuns and civil and church authorities and shows the tenacious nuns as the usual winners.

I was surprised to find two recent books by feminist historians who considered the Ursulines early champions of women's rights because they managed to work around the patriarchies of church and state to fulfill their teaching mission. For Laurence Lux-Sterritt, in *Redefining Female Religious Life*, it was the acceptance of cloister in the seventeenth century that allowed the French Ursulines to become the first congregation of religious women officially recognized by the pope as a teaching order.[3] Her extensive bibliography of both published material and unpublished dissertations suggests that she was not the only twentieth-century scholar interested in these women who successfully combined the cloister and the classroom. Emily Clark's study of the New Orleans Ursulines, *Masterless Mistresses*, documents how, even more significantly, the Ursulines shaped the intellectual and social lives of Louisiana women—whether daughters of colonists, slaves, or indigenous tribes—in the eighteenth and early nineteenth centuries, with the result that throughout the period women in Louisiana demonstrated a higher rate of literacy than women in New England.[4] *Voices from an Early American Convent*, Clark's translation of selected letters by the first New Orleans Ursulines, underscores the role played by the nuns' writings—in the form of personal letters, chronicles, and obituaries—in holding the religious community together and passing on traditions.[5]

Both my visit to the archives and my reading gave me ample material for my conference presentation. Rather than satisfying my interest in the Ur-

3. Laurence Lux-Sterritt, *Redefining Female Religious Life: French Ursulines and English Ladies in Seventeenth-Century Catholicism* (Aldershot, Eng.: Ashgate, 2005).

4. Emily Clark, *Masterless Mistresses: The New Orleans Ursulines and the Development of a New World Society, 1727–1834* (Chapel Hill: University of North Carolina Press, 2007), 117.

5. Emily Clark, ed., *Voices from an Early American Convent: Marie Madeleine Hachard and the New Orleans Ursulines, 1727–1760* (Baton Rouge: Louisiana State University Press, 2007).

sulines, however, my research only raised new questions about my elementary school education. My inability to let go of my subject was the result in part of stepping onto the campus of Ursuline Academy after more than a sixty-year absence. I was struck by how little the grounds and the school buildings had changed since my time there. I recognized the covered walkways where we girls lined up in the morning to march, two by two, into the classroom; the inner courtyard, with its simple geometric patterns of bushes and flowers, where we crowned the statue of the Virgin Mary in May; the high ceilings and transom windows that allowed air to circulate in the classrooms during the hot and humid days of late summer and early fall, before the common use of air-conditioning; and the choir gallery of the National Shrine of Our Lady of Prompt Succor, where we sang High Mass in Latin on feast days. The only apparent change was in the faculty: the black-robed nuns had ceded their place to secular teachers in street dress.

There were other questions of a pedagogical nature about my elementary education that I had formulated in the decades since becoming a classroom teacher. Why had I retained so much of what I learned as a child into adulthood? Did it have anything to do with what the nuns taught and how they taught it, or did I just have a good memory? I remember, especially, geography classes in which we studied the history, economy, and physical features of Mexico and Central and South America as carefully as the states of our own country, in part to understand more fully the boarders from Venezuela sent to Ursuline Academy for high school. Religion class involved not only memorization of catechism but stories of female saints, women like our patroness, Saint Ursula, the medieval martyr who defied the Huns; or Teresa of Ávila, mystic, activist, and Doctor of the Church. Such saints showed us how independent and strong we could become if we had the courage to follow their example. We received holy cards with their pictures as rewards for good behavior and as presents on feast days. I remember music class in which, twice a week, a sweet, older nun trained us in choral singing (even as a child I was an alto), not only the Latin hymns and liturgy we sang in church but also English and American folk songs. To this day, whenever I hear "Danny Boy," I begin to sing "Londonderry Air," the lyrics I learned for that tune at Ursuline Academy. I have always been amazed when my friends, even those who are teachers, draw a blank when I ask them what they learned in elementary school.

It was only once I started teaching and faced the difficulty of devoting equal attention to all of my students that I began to appreciate how well my

4

Ursuline teachers had accomplished this task. My elementary school classes were big, at least thirty girls per class, and yet the nuns knew every one of us. It was Mother Henrietta, my first-grade teacher, who discovered that I was nearsighted when I was unable to read the blackboard from the first row. Once I had glasses, she made sure that I wore them whenever I was in class but left them in their case when it was time for physical education. Another nun helped correct the lisp I had developed in second grade by working on my pronunciation during recess. The nuns seemed to be always with us on the playground, twirling the jump rope, pushing the swings, or joining us in a game of Simon Says. In bad weather, when we had recess inside the gymnasium, they taught those of us who didn't want to play volleyball how to knit and embroider. I remember no more serious punishments dispensed for misbehavior than having girls stand at the back of the classroom for ten or fifteen minutes. On the contrary, there were many little rewards, such as holy cards, sharpened pencils, and an occasional sucking candy, meted out for both good behavior and academic success. How had the nuns developed such successful ways to manage their classrooms?

My final question concerned the "Frenchness" of my early education. There was at least one nun from France on the faculty when I was at Ursuline Academy. In preschool and kindergarten, we had coloring books written in French, and later we learned French songs, poems, and prayers. We studied French grammar every year but neither spoke nor read the language. My ability to understand French as a child came from listening to conversations in Louisiana French between my mother and grandparents, not from my teachers. The Ursulines made much of their French connections, but so did the entire city of New Orleans. I began to wonder if there was anything distinctively French about the Ursuline curriculum and pedagogy beyond the fact that the school existed in America's best-known "French" city. Had my years with the Ursulines introduced me to the rich intellectual and artistic traditions of France that I have devoted my life to studying and teaching since my undergraduate years? I could not find answers to these questions in the history books.

The historical studies, however, mentioned a pedagogical text published by the French Ursulines in 1705 entitled *Les Règlemens des religieuses Ursulines de la Congrégation de Paris*. Clark makes only passing reference to this document brought by the Ursulines from Rouen to New Orleans in 1727, but Lux-Sterritt spends several pages on it and claims that the *Règlemens* was adopted throughout France in Ursuline schools of the seventeenth and eighteenth centuries. Heaney believes that the *Règlemens* introduced the Ursuline teaching methods to the New World.[6] I was able to obtain a digital copy of this document from the Bibliothèque nationale de France. Thanks to the miracles of modern technology, I could see on my computer screen a rare example of what Lux-Sterritt deems "the actual pedagogical work undertaken in [Ursuline] schools in the early modern era."[7] This document, moreover, had the *privilège du roi* (king's permission) and the seal of Louis XIV on the final pages to prove its authenticity. As I read the *Règlemens*, I realized that the traits I had appreciated in my Ursuline education—care from the nuns inside and outside of the classroom, individualized attention, the integration of religion and academic subjects—had been part of the Ursuline project from the time of the congregation's founding.

Two twentieth-century studies of the Ursuline teaching methods, both by Ursuline nuns, helped me understand better the nature and purpose of the *Règlemens*. Sister M. Monica's *Angela Merici and Her Teaching Idea [1474–1540]*, a lengthy exploration of the life and work of the Italian founder of the Ursulines, explains how the *Règlemens* reflects Merici's beliefs that the teacher should relate to her pupil as a mother to her child and that teachers must adapt their instruction to the needs and talents of their pupils.[8] Mother Marie de St. Jean Martin's *The Ursuline Method of Education* traces the publication history of the *Règlemens* from 1652 to 1895 and pays particular attention to the influence of the Jesuits on the Ursulines.[9]

Les Règlemens des religieuses Ursulines de la Congrégation de Paris records a milestone in French education: it is the first coherent plan for the establishment and maintenance of schools designed specifically for girls. Although relatively brief, the *Règlemens* covers every aspect of girls' education, from the grouping of girls into classes and the organization of the faculty to the subjects taught, teaching methods, and school calendar, and it does so for both the boarding school and the day school that coexisted in every convent. Although the *Règlemens* was composed and published in Paris, it was

6. See E. Clark, *Masterless Mistresses*, 56–57; Lux-Sterritt, *Redefining Female Religious Life,* 85–88; Heaney, *Century of Pioneering,* 110–13.

7. Lux-Sterritt, *Redefining Female Religious Life,* 85.

8. See especially Sister Monica's chapter 14, "Ursuline Methods of Teaching in the 17th Century," *Angela Merici and Her Teaching Idea* (New York: Longmans, Green and Co., 1927), 362–92.

9. St. Jean Martin, *The Ursuline Method of Education* (Rahway, NJ: Quinn & Boden Co., 1946).

adopted in Ursuline convents throughout France and traveled from France to Canada and the Louisiana Territory. It standardized Ursuline education in the French-speaking world. The *Règlemens* had not only a far reach but a lasting one. It survived the French Revolution and was revised and reprinted under the same title in 1860. Writing in the United States during the Second World War, Mother St. Jean Martin advocated a return to the methods of the *Règlemens* as the best means of reviving Catholic education for girls. While the original purpose of the Ursulines was to advance the Catholic faith among Frenchwomen after the sixteenth-century Wars of Religion, their *Règlemens* offered a plan for girls' education that retained its relevance in the nineteenth and twentieth centuries, in France and abroad.

The first part of this book consists of several chapters giving context and commentary on the *Règlemens*. The first chapter, entitled "The Ursulines: First Women Educators of France," provides a history of *Les Règlemens des religieuses Ursulines de la Congrégation de Paris* from the Counter-Reformation to the modern era. I begin with the creation of non-cloistered Ursuline communities in sixteenth-century Italy and end shortly before Vatican II in the 1960s and 1970s, when the Ursulines were released from the obligation of cloister. After a brief overview of women's education in early modern France, I introduce the Italian saint and founder of the Ursulines, Angela Merici, whose writings gave the French Ursulines the principal ideas for their groundbreaking teaching methods. After a summary of the establishment of the Ursuline order in Paris in the early seventeenth century, I turn my attention to the 1705 *Règlemens*. In my analysis of this text, I not only outline the organization of the schools, the curriculum, and teaching methods but also highlight parts of the *Règlemens* that will be of interest to contemporary teachers. How much autonomy did classroom teachers enjoy? What was involved in teacher training? How did the Ursuline education for girls differ from Jesuit education for boys? Were the Ursulines trying to recruit girls to the convent or prepare them for the secular world? Did their methods for teaching the French language differ from the ones we use today?

In the second chapter, I examine the revisions made to the 1705 document in the nineteenth century that resulted in the 1860 document, with the title spelled in modern French as *Règlements*. Finally, in chapter 3, I look at the twentieth century's interest in the 1860 *Règlements* as expressed most eloquently by Mother Marie de St. Jean Martin, OSU, in her *Ursuline Method of Education*, written after the Ursulines had become an international order.

7

In my study of all three books, I attempt to situate Ursuline pedagogy in a historical framework. I discuss the history of the order itself; the history of girls' education in France; the Catholic Church's stance on education in the seventeenth, nineteenth, and twentieth centuries; the conflicts between church and state over education; and the changes in the curricula offered in Catholic schools for girls from the late Renaissance in Europe until the end of the nineteenth century.

In my commentary, I also hope to demonstrate the long-neglected importance of the Ursulines in the intellectual life of early modern France. Composed collaboratively by mother superiors of the Paris convents and their noble patronesses, with the advice of priests and bishops, the *Règlemens* was never signed by any author. One consequence of this absence of an author's name has been the incorrect attribution of the title "première éducatrice de France" (first woman educator of France) to Mme de Maintenon, second wife of Louis XIV, who founded a boarding school for the daughters of poor nobility at Saint Cyr in 1684. Mme de Maintenon, however, was herself a pupil of the Paris Ursulines, whose boarding schools existed five decades before her Maison Royale de St. Louis. The Ursulines deserve credit not only for establishing schools but also for participating in the democratization of education in France. The *Règlemens* describes how they served the daughters of the poor and lower classes in day schools that existed alongside boarding schools for the nobility and bourgeoisie without challenging contemporary standards of class and gender. Finally, the *Règlemens* suggests the vital role the Ursulines played in the spread of literacy during the seventeenth and eighteenth centuries.[10]

The *Règlemens* reflects the intellectual arguments of early modern France. It recalls Descartes's *Discourse on Method* of 1737 in its insistence that knowledge must be based on irrefutable principles. The Ursuline version of Descartes's "cogito" is the "Mother Idea" of their foundress Angela Merici, which simply asserts that mothers are the most effective educators of young children. We find the attempt to re-create the mother-daughter relationship in the Ursuline schools in every chapter of the *Règlemens*, from those dealing with the daily routines of boarders to instruction in sewing and penmanship. The *Règlemens* has its roots in the Counter-Reformation and has much to teach us about the practical application of Counter-Reformation devotional treatises.

10. André Chervel, *Histoire de l'enseignement du français du XVII au XX siècle* (Paris: Éditions Retz, 2006), 43.

8

Throughout its chapters, we hear echoes of François de Sales's *Introduction à la vie dévote* (Introduction to the Devout Life) of 1609, the treatise on piety that sought to enlist secular women in the church's effort to re-proselytize France. In the chapters on religious instruction, we note the influence of Ignatius of Loyola's *Spiritual Exercises* of 1548, which served as a guidebook for lay Christians striving to make prayer and devotion a part of their daily lives. Chapters on catechism instruction that cite the writings of sixteenth-century clerics from France, Italy, and Spain as sources of inspiration for lesson plans indicate that the Ursuline founders studied Counter-Reformation thought from throughout Europe. In the domain of pedagogy, St. Jean Martin has documented the close connections between the founders of the Paris congregation and the Jesuits, who had composed the *Ratio studiorum* (Plan of Studies) of 1599, the first standardized system of Catholic education for boys.[11] This engagement with contemporary Catholic discussions of education is a distinguishing feature not only of the 1705 *Règlemens* but also of the 1860 revised edition and St. Jean Martin's 1946 defense of the Ursuline method.

Girls' education becomes a major theme in French literature from the mid-seventeenth until the mid-nineteenth century. Two of Molière's most popular comedies, *L'École des femmes* (School for Wives) of 1662 and *Les Femmes savantes* (The Learned Women) of 1672, address the dangers of an inadequate education as well as of one that is too erudite. The importance of mothers in preparing girls for life in secular society was an obsession the Ursulines shared with women writers of the French classical period. In the mid-seventeenth century, the letters of Mme de Sévigné to her married daughter demonstrate Sévigné's belief in a mother's lifelong influence on her daughter's social and spiritual development. Mme de Lafayette's psychological novel, *La Princesse de Clèves* of 1678, is, in major part, a study of a mother's ability to instill principles that will fortify her daughter against the dissolute life of the royal court. In the mid-eighteenth century, Enlightenment writers composed novels that were highly critical not only of Catholicism in general but also of convents and the education they provided. The best-known treatments of this subject, Choderlos de Laclos's *Les Liaisons dangereuses* (Dangerous Liaisons) of 1782 and Denis Diderot's *La Religieuse* (The Nun) of 1792, either see the convent as a place of perversion and imprisonment or condemn convent education as a system for keeping girls in ignorance and

11. See St. Jean Martin, *Ursuline Method*, appendix A, "Origin and Development of the Method of Education of the Ursulines," 285–320.

juvenility. Gustave Flaubert's *Madame Bovary* of 1857 adds a twist to the Enlightenment criticism by suggesting that a convent education stimulates the passions as well as the world-weariness we associate with Romantic ennui. In my discussion of the 1860 *Règlements,* I have compared, when appropriate, these novelistic portrayals of convent life to the one we find in the Ursuline rule. Readers will find that both the 1705 and 1860 regulations paint a much more positive picture of convent education, one that suggests the novelists I have mentioned were informed more by misguided views than fact.

I have quoted often from all three books that I analyze. I have cited the 1705 text, in modernized French spelling, to give the reader an idea of the style and vocabulary of the original document. At times, I have cited the 1860 text to demonstrate the nineteenth-century Ursulines' fidelity to the principles and style of the 1705 original, but I have also cited the sections that vary significantly from the original. As for *The Ursuline Method of Education,* written in English, I could not resist sharing with twenty-first-century teachers St. Jean Martin's forceful, well-researched arguments for a return to the methods of her Ursuline forebears. I do not think I am alone in finding much writing on pedagogy off-putting by its terminology and wordiness. St. Jean Martin proves that a teaching manual need never be boring.

Following these chapters is my translation of the 1705 *Règlemens.* I decided against including the original French text with my translation because the poor condition of the document makes it difficult to read. Scholars interested in a digitized copy of the original can obtain one from the Bibliothèque nationale de France. To help anyone who wishes to locate this document in the BnF catalog, I have included the catalog number in the first footnote to the 1705 *Règlemens.*

My translation makes this long-ignored text available in English to readers interested in the history of education, especially girls' education, in Europe and America. Educators will easily recognize the *Règlemens* as a pedagogical document that, although written over three hundred years ago, is organized much like modern faculty and student handbooks. It begins with a mission statement explaining the purpose of Ursuline schools and justifying the regulations. It is arranged in chapters, which are further subdivided into articles and paragraphs dedicated to the responsibilities of all members of the school community, from the administrators of both boarding and day schools to the pupils themselves. The *Règlemens* also functions as a teaching manual, with detailed directions for the instruction of all subjects in the curriculum.

It presents a floor plan for constructing a convent that houses two separate schools and acts as a guidebook for cloistered nuns in their interactions with the secular world. To reflect the many dimensions of the *Règlemens*, I decided to translate every line of the original French and to copy the exact organization of the 1705 text into books, parts, chapters, and paragraphs. The only stylistic change I have made is to break up very long sentences, complicated by multiple clauses, some of which take up an entire paragraph. I have cut these into two or more shorter sentences to make them more readable for an English-language audience.

My greatest challenge has been finding English vocabulary to translate French words that have radically changed their meaning over three centuries or have become obsolete. I have been able to give an appropriate English translation for all vocabulary except *en semaine* and *dixainières*, terms with a particular meaning in the *Règlemens*. These two terms I have left in French and explained in footnotes. I have also translated the title, *Règlemens*, as "Regulations," rather than "Rules," to avoid confusion with other foundational Ursuline documents. The 1651 *privilège du roi* appending the *Règlemens* includes, among other writings the Ursulines had permission to publish, the *Règles et constitutions* (Rules and Constitutions) of the order. The *Règle* refers to the monastic Rule of Saint Augustine, which the Ursulines adopted when they accepted cloister. This short document explains how the nuns were to live as a fraternal community and carry out their vows of poverty, chastity, and obedience.[12] The title "Regulations" will help distinguish the *Règlemens* from this *Règle*. Because the 1705 text was revised using modern French spelling and republished in 1860, I use the spelling *Règlemens* for the original text and the modern spelling *Règlements* for the 1860 text to establish a clear distinction between these two editions.

I have added notes explaining all changes in meaning or special uses of a word. I have done the same for the titles of the Latin prayers and hymns that occur frequently in the chapters on the sacraments and daily devotions. In addition to these clarifications, I have included many other notes explaining Catholic liturgy, devotional practices, and social customs that twenty-first-century readers will be as unlikely to understand as I was until I researched the subjects. Using footnotes rather than parenthetical explanations makes the translation read more smoothly, as does breaking up the long

---

12. *Règle de Nostre Père Saint Augustin* (Paris: Jean Henault, 1657).

THREE CENTURIES OF GIRLS' EDUCATION

French sentences into shorter, more direct ones in English. To my surprise and pleasure, it was not an impossible task to render the French original into English, a phenomenon I attribute more to the Ursulines' skill as writers than to my skill as translator. Their precise, concrete language, rich in details and observations on human behavior, fits admirably Nicolas Boileau's description of the French neoclassical style: "Ce que l'on conçoit bien s'énonce claire- ment" (What is well conceived is clearly expressed).[13]

Although I have briefly addressed in the commentary the authorship and publication history of both the 1705 *Règlemens* and the 1860 revised edition, the two dates of publication, one given at the beginning of the 1705 docu- ment, the other at the end, merit further explanation. The 1705 date appears on the title page. However, after both the first and second books, we find a letter approving these *Règlemens* from the mother superior of the two Paris convents, signed by the vicar-general of the archbishop of Paris, dated 1652. Immediately following this letter, there appears Louis XIV's *privilège du roi*, giving the Ursulines of Paris exclusive rights for ten years to publish this and all other documents related to the establishment of their congregation and the functioning of their schools. It is dated March 1, 1704. The initial lines of this *privilège* explain that a new letter of permission is necessary because the original publication rights granted to the Ursulines in 1651 in perpetuum had been revoked by the king's council in August 1702. Neither the title page nor the letters tell us what the relationship is between the 1705 text and any earlier edition or why we find no copies of an edition published in the early 1650s.

Of the three Ursuline scholars who write about the *Règlemens*, Sister Jane Frances Heaney does not mention the conflicting dates because she is con- cerned not with the original Ursulines of Paris but with the New Orleans Ursulines, who brought the 1705 document with them to the New World in 1727, by which time the 1705 edition had become standard in France.[14] Sister Monica believes that the 1705 document was the earliest edition printed for public distribution and that the 1652 text was only printed for private use in the two Parisian convents.[15] Mother St. Jean Martin convincingly argues that the 1705 *Règlemens* is a reprinting, without revisions, of the 1652 text men-

13. Nicolas Boileau, *L'Art poétique*, Chant I, *Oeuvres complètes de Boileau* (Paris: Hachette, 1871–72).

14. Similarly, Emily Clark, who also only writes about the New Orleans's Ursulines, does not question the publication date of 1705.

15. Sister Monica, *Angela Merici*, 362.

tioned in the mother superior's letter of approbation: "This [1652] edition is not available today, but the [1705] edition that followed it must be identical, since the only ecclesiastical approbation that appears in it is a reproduction of that first edition, signed by H.F.H. Feret, Vicar General of the Archbishop of Paris and the Superior of the two monasteries of that city. Whereas the 'privilège du Roi,' is dated 1704, because, as it says, the letters of perpetual privilege that had been accorded July 1, 1651, were declared null and void by Arrêt with his [the king's] council, August 13, 1703."[16] Any revisions would have required a new letter of approbation from the superior of the Paris convents as well as the approval of the local bishopric. This was the case with the 1860 *Règlements*, which includes letters of approbation from bishops throughout France as well as from the Ursuline superiors. The early-eighteenth-century Parisian Ursulines would have had no trouble understanding that the *approbation* and *privilège du roi* authorized the Parisian Ursulines only to reissue the 1652 version, and St. Jean Martin is justified in calling the 1705 document "the second edition of the same [1652] *Règlemens*."

The 1652 publication date demonstrates that the *Règlemens* was a foundational document, as important to the early Ursulines as the constitutions of their order. Why, then, do no copies of the 1652 *Règlemens* exist?[17] One explanation is the destruction of religious property during the French Revolution. We know that the two original Paris convents were razed and any archives destroyed with the buildings. Yet other Ursuline documents that were published before 1652, such as the constitutions of 1640, survived the Revolution. The 1704 *privilège du roi* points to another reason for the 1652 text's disappearance: since the 1705 edition was a faithful replica of the original, there was no need to keep copies of the earlier regulations, and strict conformity to the king's decrees no doubt pleased both the monarch and episcopal authorities.

The *Règlemens* of 1705 is composed of two separate books. The first book, "De ce qui concerne l'instruction des jeunes filles" (The Education of Girls), deals with schools and teaching methods; the second book, "Des règlemens

16. St. Jean Martin, *Ursuline Method*, 294.

17. In her bibliography, Lux-Sterritt gives the publication date for *Les Règlemens des religieuses Ursulines de la Congrégation de Paris* as 1651. Her source, the Archives Départementales de la Haute Garonne, which houses the documents of the Ursulines of Toulouse, undoubtedly copied this date from the *privilège du roi* found in the 1705 edition. The *Règlemens* could not have been published before 1652, when the archbishop of Paris and the mother superior gave their approval. Moreover, the page numbers cited by Lux-Sterritt from the *Règlemens* correspond exactly to the page numbers in the 1705 edition.

communs du monastère" (The Regulations of the Monastic Community), treats the monastic life. The second book, like the first, is organized by chapters and paragraphs that appoint the hours of rising, sleeping, prayer, meals, and recreation as well as the order of devotional exercises. The second book is also very detailed and gives precise descriptions of clothing, meals, and even the punishments the mother superior could impose for misdeeds. It begins with a mission statement asserting the need for rules that enable the nuns to fulfill their vows of poverty, chastity, and obedience. While these two books complement each other, they exist as independent texts. The first book does not talk about the monastic community; in fact, it forbids the teaching faculty to discuss convent life with pupils. The second book says little about the schools. The two books have not always been published together. There exists a separate edition of the monastic regulations, published in 1653 under the slightly different title *Règlemens pour les religieuses de saincte Ursule de la congrégation de Paris.*[18] In the nineteenth century, the second book disappeared completely from the revised *Règlements* of 1860. Although the second book is not essential to our study of the Ursuline teaching methods, I have cited certain of its chapters in my commentary because they provide valuable information, such as a list of the books read by the nuns both in community and individually. This list is not found in the regulations on education.[19] Citing the regulations of the monastic community also allows me to acknowledge the Ursuline commitment to the religious life as well as to teaching.

18. The publishers of the two books are also different. The first book was published by Louis Josse, while the second book was published by Gilles Blaizot, who also published the Ursuline *Constitutions* in 1640.

19. The Ursulines were prolific writers and often repeated the same themes in different documents. Scholars of monastic life can find the same information on the monastic community contained in the second book of the 1705 *Règlemens* in the *Constitutions des religieuses de Sainte Ursule de la Congrégation de Paris* (Paris: chez Gilles Blaizot, près la Porte Saint Michel, 1640).

THE
Ursulines
*First
Women Educators
of France*

ALTHOUGH THE FRENCH RENAISSANCE PRODUCED IMPORTANT
treatises on education, we find little reflection on the specific needs of girls
from the best-known French authors of the sixteenth century. Rabelais's educational utopia, the Abbaye de Thélème of *Gargantua*, is little more than
a secularized, co-ed monastery where men and women, all highborn and
already possessing advanced knowledge of the fine arts, literature, and foreign
languages, pass their time in intellectual pursuits and physical games until
they leave the monastery to marry. Montaigne's educational program, outlined in "De l'institution des enfans" (On the Education of Children) (*Essais*
I, xxvi), which stresses the formation of judgment rather than memory, is
dedicated to the Countess Diane de Foix but was clearly intended for male
children of the nobility.

Mme de Maintenon, second wife of Louis XIV, usually receives credit
for having created the first school for girls in France in the final decades of
the seventeenth century. Her Maison Royale de St. Louis, a boarding school
for the daughters of the poor nobility, was established at St. Cyr in 1684 and
continued to function until the French Revolution. At St. Cyr, girls were
separated into classes according to age and were taught a curriculum that
prepared them for life in the secular world. Their training included domestic

arts, such as regulating household finances, the art of conversation in social gatherings, as well as reading, writing, and computation.[1] François Fénelon, Mme de Maintenon's spiritual director, shares her reputation as a pioneer in girls' education. In 1687, three years after the foundation of the Maison Royale, he composed *De l'education des filles* (The Education of Girls), a treatise that recognized the essential role women play in society and justified their right to an education equal to that offered men. Like Mme de Maintenon, Fénelon intended a practical education for girls of the nobility; unlike her, he saw the mother as the primary teacher of children and the home as the most important classroom. A mother was to form her daughter's character by modeling virtuous behavior as well as teaching the fundamentals of language arts and arithmetic through play and gentle direction.[2]

While Mme de Maintenon deserves credit for advancing women's education in France, the title of "premières éducatrices de France" (first women educators of France) more rightly goes to the Companies and Congregations of Saint Ursula—the Ursulines—who started educating girls in France at the turn of the seventeenth century. The Ursulines served the urban poor, peasants, and orphans in city and country, as well as the wealthy and noble, almost a century before Mme de Maintenon created the Maison Royale. Well before Fénelon, the Ursulines recognized the role of mothers in education. Mme de Maintenon, who was herself educated in Ursuline convents in Niort and Paris and later became the financial patron of an Ursuline convent school in Rueil near Paris, imitated the Ursuline model in composing her teaching faculty and in grouping girls according to age.[3] Ursuline schools not only preceded St. Cyr but survived far longer than Maintenon's project, expanding beyond Europe to attain notable successes in the French colonies of North America in the eighteenth and nineteenth centuries.

The Ursulines represented an intermediate step from the cloistered condition of medieval nuns to the active roles of teachers, nurses, and social workers we associate with modern Catholic religious congregations. At their origin in Counter-Reformation Italy, the Ursulines were not cloistered. The members of the Company of Saint Ursula, founded by Angela Merici and approved by

---

1. Jacques Prévot, *Première éducatrice de France. Madame de Maintenon* (Paris: Éditions Belin, 1981), 1–30.

2. François Fénelon, *De l'Education des filles*, Athena e-texts, accessed July 11, 2019, http://athena.unige.ch/athena/fenelon/fenelon-education-des-filles.html.

3. Prévot, *Première éducatrice de France*, 20–21.

the bishop of Brescia in 1536, took private vows of poverty, chastity, and obedience. They did not wear habits and lived with their families. They worked
in public places, often town squares, caring for the physical needs of women
and children and instructing girls in catechism, prayer, and church liturgy.
Non-enclosure was so essential to Angela's mission that she sought papal
recognition as "an uncloistered virginity, canonically protected," which Paul
III's bull of 1544 granted to her company of women in perpetuity.[4] When the
Ursulines first established themselves in the South of France, they retained
their secular status. In 1612, however, the majority of French Ursulines chose
to become cloistered orders. The Bull of Approbation signed by Pope Paul V
gave the Ursulines the right, never before granted to a Catholic women's
congregation, to add a fourth vow of teaching to the three traditional vows of
poverty, chastity, and obedience. This fourth vow allowed them to bring not
only boarders into their convents, as nuns had done throughout the Middle
Ages, but also day pupils—that is, poor girls living with their families who
had limited hours for study. Sister Monica makes a convincing argument
that the Ursulines, who observed cloister but received the secular world into
their convents, set a precedent that would allow future orders like the Sisters
of Charity to go into the world as they fulfilled their mission of ministering to
the poor.[5] The French Ursulines became the first Catholic women's missionary order. Their teaching vocation made it possible to receive permission to
travel to Quebec, Canada, in 1639, where they supported the Jesuits' efforts
to convert indigenous tribes to Catholicism. Less than a century later, in 1727,
twelve Ursulines from Rouen created the first girls' school in the Louisiana
Territory, the Ursuline Academy of New Orleans, today the oldest continuously operating school for girls in the United States.

From the time of Angela Merici, during the late Italian Renaissance, the
Ursulines found direction in documents composed by their founders that
defined their educational goals, accounted for teacher preparation, and considered the needs of different student populations. Merici's simple advice to
her companions contained the seeds of a teaching method that would later
be developed by her French heirs in *Les Règlemens des religieuses Ursulines
de la Congrégation de Paris* (1652, 1705). French Ursulines brought these regulations with them to Quebec in 1639 and New Orleans in 1727. Ursuline

4. Sister Monica, *Angela Merici*, 181, 84–107, 237.
5. Ibid., 342–43.

congregations in France remained faithful to the 1705 document throughout the eighteenth century until the French Revolution forced the dissolution of religious congregations. When congregations returned to France in the nineteenth century, contemporary Ursulines revised the 1705 document to address the needs of a new age but without abandoning the principles of the original document. Even in the twentieth century, after separate Ursuline congregations came together to form the Roman Union and established convent schools throughout the world, their prioress general defended the universal and timeless value of the French regulations of 1705 and 1860 as the most effective method of educating girls.

ANGELA MERICI AND THE ORIGINS OF THE *RÈGLEMENS*

The *Règlemens* had its origin in the *Regola della Compagnia di S. Orsola*, composed by Angela Merici circa 1525 and approved by Pope Paul III as the official rule for the non-cloistered women of the Company of Saint Ursula in 1544, four years after Merici's death. Thanks to Sister Monica, who has compiled all available information about Angela's youth, we know that she was born into a peasant family near Brescia, Italy. She had no formal education but could nevertheless read both Italian and Latin. She was unable to write—a lack of skill not unusual in her time—but had a secretary record the documents she composed. Her father, a landowner and farmer, was literate and read to his children at night from Scripture, the lives of the saints, and the sayings of the early Christian monks.[6] Just as many children today learn to read before entering school through an early exposure to books, so also Angela became literate in her home. Like any Catholic child from a devout family in late-fifteenth-century Italy, Angela acquired a familiarity with the Scripture, church history, dogma, sacred music, art, and the rudiments of Latin simply by attending mass regularly and participating in the many ceremonies and sacraments that filled the liturgical year. The more practical arts—simple arithmetic, hygiene, cooking, caring for the sick, supervising children—Angela learned in the home from her mother and the aunts she lived with after her parents died. When she decided in her adolescence to care for the women and children victimized by the Italian wars of the 1490s

---

6. Ibid., II, 29. Sister Monica gives the name of Nazari, a Brescian notary who, working from depositions, compiled the earliest account of Merici's life.

and, moreover, to use the opportunity to teach girls to read prayer books and catechism, she had already been educated without ever spending a day in a schoolroom.

Of the three documents Angela dictated to her secretary, the *Regola* [*Rule*] *of Angela Merici* and her *Counsels* are most relevant to her educational project.[7] The *Rule* explains the organization of the Company of Saint Ursula, a community named after the fourth-century virgin and martyr, and lays out the objectives and values that justify the community's existence, in the manner of a mission statement. The prologue praises teaching as a divinely inspired vocation, open to all chaste and pious women committed to the propagation of the Catholic faith regardless of their age, wealth, social status, or even educational level. This initial declaration of openness set the tone for an egalitarian and practical document.

The community had governing officers, but these officers were elected by the members rather than appointed by bishops or priests. The *Rule* concentrates on the division of work within the community, such as the training of novices, the organization of schools, communication with local laypeople, and the oversight of finances, rather than on the delegation of authority. The highest officer, the mother general, was chosen for her piety and tenderness toward her companions, "so that with maternal compassion she may be quick to help [the daughters of the community] in all their wants."[8] Biweekly neighborhood assemblies of the members ensured the airing and resolution of problems. While officially the bishop retained the authority to change or even dissolve the community, it operated independently under the guidance of the *Rule*. The *Rule* also outlined a simple method of teacher training. The teachers, known as mistresses, formed the novices, instructing them both in the community's devotional practices and pedagogy.

The ability to read was the most important skill the mistress could impart to novices. If a novice could not read, a mistress taught her to do so. The mistresses were expected to act lovingly toward the young women they trained, "striving to enfold [the novices] in a maternal tenderness" that involved caring

7. The original manuscript of the *Regola* was lost after the 1770 canonization process of Angela Merici (see Centro Studi Internazionali Santa Angela e Sant'Orsola website, accessed December 14, 2021, www.angelamerici.it/index_dettagli.php?get_id=57. The *Counsels* were published with Merici's *Testament* (see Sister Monica, *Angela Merici*, 201). My citations of these two documents all come from Sister Monica's translations of the two documents.

8. Sister Monica, *Angela Merici*, 258.

for their physical needs, learning their individual talents and limitations, and practicing guidance and patience. Of the actual subjects the teachers were expected to master, the *Rule* only mentions Christian doctrine and preparation for the sacraments. Otherwise, the *Rule* simply directs the mistresses to model the "good conduct" of a pious woman who interacts daily with the secular world.[9]

In the *Rule*, the model for the Company of Saint Ursula is the family, and the model for the teacher is the mother. The *Rule* introduces us to what Sister Monica has termed the "Mother Idea," the foundational principle of Merici's teaching method and one that put her at odds with the male writers of her time. The most famous educational treatises of the Renaissance—Machiavelli's *The Prince* and Erasmus's *Education of a Christian Prince*—made little mention of women, much less their education.[10] According to Sister Monica, they were not alone among the Italian humanists, who saw the mother-educator as a threat to paternal authority: "Consciously or unconsciously, Angela Merici's movement in Brescia was a reactionary reform against the pagan ideals imported through the humanists into the education of girls. Her movement may be clearly defined as a reaction in which the Mother-idea according to Christian tradition was to be re-emphasized and made workable."[11] The Bible and the lives of the saints offered a heroic version of womanhood, especially in the figure of the Virgin Mary, the ideal mother portrayed in Renaissance paintings caring for the Christ Child. Merici's personal experience as "a daughter of the people" confirmed her belief that the mother, in daily contact with the child, was best suited to form the child's character.

The Mother Idea is made more explicit in the *Counsels* Merici dictated for her followers before her death. These short statements do not present any set curriculum or pedagogical method, both of which are left to the teachers' initiative and good judgment. The *Counsels* more closely resemble maxims in which Merici exhorts her daughters to set a good example for the girls they educate by transforming the school into a loving home. She urges them to get to know each pupil, show flexibility, be slow to punish, encourage cooperation, instill the love of God and neighbor by incorporating devotion

9. Ibid., 263–67.

10. Erasmus was not against women's education, but he did not think it had much practical value since women had no role in society outside of the family (J. K. Sowards, "Erasmus and the Education of Women," *Sixteenth Century Journal* 13, no. 4 (Winter 1982): 77–89.

11. Sister Monica, *Angela Merici*, 197.

and charity into daily activities, and set high standards for intellectual and moral achievement. By appealing to the young girls' innate ability to reason, Merici believed that teachers facilitated the development of self-control and, with it, self-confidence and independence.[12]

Many of the pedagogical ideas in the *Rule* and the *Counsels* are commonplaces of Renaissance thought. Rabelais, Merici's contemporary, as well as Montaigne, who wrote a half-century later, understood the importance of early education and of the pedagogue's need to teach through example. Like Rabelais and Montaigne, Merici denounced corporal punishment and forced learning. The *Rules*, as much as Rabelais's "Lettre à Gargantua" (Letter to Gargantua) in *Pantagruel* (1532) or Montaigne's essay "De l'institution des enfans" (1580), advocate an education that cares for the body as well as the mind and stresses literacy and reasoning over rote memorization. All three thinkers believed that the goal of education was to prepare the young person for life in secular society. Merici, however, was not a humanist who drew her inspiration from pre-Christian classical Greek and Roman literature. Tutored, rather, by the teachings of the New Testament and her observations of human behavior, she developed a pedagogy that sought not only to develop a girl's mind but also to strengthen her will as a means of countering the weaknesses of human nature. Nothing was more important to Merici than the Mother Idea, which she tried to instill in her followers through the counsels included in her last will and testament.[13] Yet she was also prescient in realizing that for her community to endure, it must have the freedom to govern itself as well as to change according to place and circumstance. The 1544 Bull of Approbation from Pope Paul III recognizes this privilege: "[That the Company of Saint Ursula] might be endued with the power to yield to the exigencies of the time and suit itself to the needs of each age."[14]

ESTABLISHMENT OF THE URSULINES IN FRANCE

Although the Ursulines began in Italy, they developed into a religious congregation in France. In 1592, Françoise de Bermond, a devout French Catholic who observed Merici's rule for laywoman catechists, received authoriza-

12. Ibid., 203–14.
13. Ibid., 300. Writing in 1927, Sister Monica rightly noted that the majority of twentieth-century Ursuline schools were "still stamped with this special characteristic."
14. Ibid., 238.

tion from Pope Clement VIII to establish Ursuline schools in the region of Avignon.[15] The migration of the Ursulines from Italy to southern France was not surprising, given the geographical proximity of the two areas and the fact that Protestantism had gained a strong foothold in the South of France, while Avignon had remained a Roman Catholic enclave during the Wars of Religion. The Jesuits had already established an institution for boys there in 1565.[16] Bermond's initiative encouraged the establishment of Ursuline communities throughout the South of France. According to Emily Clark, there were almost thirty such Companies of Saint Ursula by 1610.[17] Impressed by Bermond's success, in 1610 devout noblewomen living in Paris invited her to establish Ursuline communities and schools in the capital.[18]

Lux-Sterritt, who chronicles the seventeenth-century Ursulines' establishment and expansion in France, explains that the original French Ursulines lived and worked no differently than their Italian predecessors: "The first Ursulines were therefore more than a simple lay sorority, since they lived in a community with its own hierarchy and regulations; nonetheless, they were emphatically not nuns, since they took no solemn vows and did not observe strict enclosure."[19] Bermond and her French sisters, however, faced a completely different political situation than did Merici's company. In the final decade of the sixteenth century, the Counter-Reformation was at its height. The Council of Trent (1545–63), which embodied the Catholic Church's response to Protestantism, required all female religious to be cloistered, even if it was their vocation to minister to the poor and teach the laity.[20] Moreover, groups of unmarried women who worked in the streets and public squares of French cities aroused the distrust of noble and bourgeois families who might

15. There is disagreement over the date and place of the first Ursuline school in France. Sister Monica cites 1594 as the year when Bermond received Clement VIII's *Missio Canonica* and established a school at l'Isle-sur-la-Sorgue (ibid., 336). St. Jean Martin also gives the place as l'Isle-sur-la-Sorgue but the date as 1596 (*Ursuline Method*, 289). Lux-Sterritt gives the date as 1592 and the place as Avignon (*Redefining Female Religious Life*, 3).

16. "Histoire d'Avignon," Horizon Provence, accessed July 9, 2020, https://www.horizon-provence .com/histoire-avignon/11_guerres-religion-avignon.htm#:~:text=Pendant%20la%20seconde %20moiti%C3%A9%20du,nord%20dans%20le%20Dauphin%C3%A9%20voisin.

17. E. Clark, *Masterless Mistresses*, 21.

18. Sister Monica, *Angela Merici*, 336–41. It was Mme de Sainte-Beuve who issued the invitation.

19. Lux-Sterritt, *Redefining Female Religious Life*, 20–21.

20. See Decrees of the Council of Trent, session 25 (Papal Encyclicals Online, accessed August 29, 2018, papalencyclicals.net/councils/trent.htm).

have served as financial patrons.[21] In an effort to reconcile their mission with church demands and to allay social fears, the leaders of the Ursuline communities in Paris sought permission to become a religious order but not follow the traditional model of monastic life. They agreed to cloister while insisting upon the right to receive girls into the convent for the purpose of teaching them. Ecclesiastical authorities were quick to accept the offer of services that would help spread the Catholic faith in France. In 1612, Pope Paul V officially recognized the Ursulines of the Congregation of Paris as a new religious order required to observe, along with the three traditional solemn vows of poverty, chastity, and obedience, a fourth solemn vow of instruction. The 1612 papal bull also repeated the privilege granted to Merici by Pope Paul III to adapt the means of carrying out this fourth vow as circumstances demanded.[22] The Ursuline nuns of the Congregation of Paris thus became the first women's religious order with the right, officially granted by the Vatican, to incorporate schools into their convents.

Once the new order had received papal authorization, the queen regent of France, Marie de Medici, promoted its efforts, and cloistered Ursuline congregations spread throughout France. Lux-Sterritt has traced the existence of over three hundred Ursuline houses in all parts of France by the end of the seventeenth century.[23] This outreach was not limited to the French territory. Less than a half-century after the order's formation, Jesuits, who saw the Ursulines living under the rule of the Congregation of Paris as kindred spirits, invited the nuns to support their missionary efforts in the New World.[24] In 1639, French Ursulines traveled to Quebec, where they created a convent school for indigenous girls, the first girls' school in North America.

To become a religious order, the Ursulines were obliged to adopt the rule of a recognized monastic community.[25] They chose the fifth-century rule of Saint Augustine because they believed that its simple requirements for prayer, fasting, and discipline would allow them the time and strength to

---

21. There were other problems explored by Lux-Sterritt, such as the question of financing the schools, the inability to attract girls from the nobility and upper-middle class to a situation that was neither cloister nor marriage, and the desire of some Ursuline communities to give more importance to prayer and devotional exercises (Lux-Sterritt, *Redefining Female Religious Life*, 34–45).

22. Sister Monica, *Angela Merici*, 342.

23. Lux-Sterritt, *Redefining Female Religious Life*, 208.

24. Heaney, *Century of Pioneering*, 20–22.

25. The Council of Trent forbade the creation of new religious orders.

teach.[26] The rule served as the basis of the 1640 *Constitution des religieuses de Saincte Ursule de la Congrégation de Paris*, which formally established the order.[27] In 1652, the Ursulines further published *Les Règlemens des religieuses Ursulines de la Congrégation de Paris*, a document in two books, of which the first book is devoted entirely to schools and teaching methods. The *privilège du roi* of Louis XIV granted the Ursulines of Paris "le privilège perpétual . . . pour l'impression des Livres à l'usage de leur ordre" (the right in perpetuity to print books for the use of their order).[28] The first book of the *Règlemens* soon proved popular beyond the walls of the original convent on the rue St. Jacques. After it was approved by the archbishop of Paris in 1652 and later reauthorized for publication by Louis XIV in 1704, Ursuline congregations in other parts of France adopted these regulations with the approval of their local bishop.[29] Such was the case of the Rouen Ursulines, who carried the *Règlemens* with them when they sailed to New Orleans in 1727.

THE COUNTER-REFORMATION AND THE URSULINES

The Ursulines were an order born of the Counter-Reformation. As such, they reflect in both their spirit and teaching methods the Counter-Reformation impetus to form Catholic men and women who would lead society away from Protestantism. The French Ursulines became a religious congregation in the midst of the seventeenth-century devotional movement that took on "the delicate and demanding task of rebuilding a trusting relationship between the people and their Church, working daily in the world to strengthen the links between secular and religious."[30] The most influential writer of this movement in France was the bishop of Geneva, François de Sales. Sister Monica

26. Lux-Sterritt, *Redefining Female Religious Life*, 69.

27. *Constitution des religieuses de Saincte Ursule de la Congrégation de Paris* (Paris: Gilles Blaizor, 1640). The first pages of the 1640 Constitution indicate that it is a revision of an earlier version of the constitutions of the Parisian congregation. We have no record of this earlier document. The 1640 Constitution is preceded by the *Règle de Notre Père Saint Augustin* (The Rule of Our Father Saint Augustine).

28. This *privilège* was the equivalent of the modern copyright, although no money was involved, and explains why we find the *Règlemens de la Congregation de Paris* used in Ursuline convents in other parts of France.

29. Such was the case of the Ursulines of Toulouse studied by Lux-Sterritt. Sister Monica points out that communities of Primitive Ursulines, that is, who did not accept cloister, often existed in the same cities as monastic Ursulines, although the majority of French Ursulines quickly accepted cloister and the advantages cloister brought to their teaching mission (*Angela Merici*, 343–49).

30. Lux-Sterritt, *Redefining Female Religious Life*, 18.

has outlined de Sales's interest in the Company of Saint Ursula, especially in its success in "combating false teachings," that is, Protestantism. He voiced initial opposition to cloister as well, as unfitting for religious women whose mission required free movement in the world.[31] Sister Monica finds similarities between Merici's Mother Idea and de Sales's attempts to highlight the maternal elements of church teachings, such as care of the poor. De Sales recognized that the Ursulines shared his belief in the possibility of leading a pious life in the secular world: "[His] message was an exhortation for the mystically minded not to shrink from the concrete world but, on the contrary, to anchor their existence (including secular concerns) in religion."[32]

De Sales is only mentioned once in the 1705 *Règlemens*, and this reference is to his writings on the sacrament of penance.[33] Yet we find many similarities between *L'Introduction à la vie dévote* (Introduction to the Devout Life) of 1608, de Sales's most consequential work, and the Ursuline *Règlemens*, probably because the founders of the Congregation of Paris and de Sales shared a common interest in a new form of devotional life. The originality of de Sales's work lay in its assertion that married women and mothers could achieve piety in the secular world by practicing the simple virtues of domestic life, such as the care of children, service to the poor and sick, and the efficient management of the household. He addressed laywomen of all social conditions "ès villes, ès ménages, en la cour" (living in cities, in charge of households, at the royal court), assuring them that it was possible to embrace piety and the world:

Ainsi peut une âme vigoureuse et constante vivre au monde sans recevoir aucune humeur mondaine, trouver des sources d'une douce piété au milieu des ondes amères de ce siècle, et voler entre les flammes des convoitises terrestres sans brûler les ailes des sacrés désirs de la vie dévote.

Thus, a vigorous and resolute soul can live in the world without acquiring a worldly temperament, can find fountains of sweet piety in the middle of the bitter seas of this century, and can fly through the

31. Once the Ursulines of Paris accepted cloister, de Sales endorsed their action and even encouraged the Sisters of the Visitation to do the same (Sister Monica, *Angela Merici*, 329–32, 347–48).

32. Lux-Sterritt, *Redefining Female Religious Life*, 18.

33. See first part, chapter five, section IV, paragraph 2, in which the *Véritable conduite de Saint François de Sales pour la confession et la communion* is mentioned as one of many books the class mistresses could use to help them prepare girls for confession.

flames of earthly covetousness without singeing the wings of the sacred desires of a devout life.[34]

He pointed out numerous opportunities for women to set an example of virtue
for their husbands and children by avoiding idleness, gossip, and adultery but
also by cultivating moderation in their treatment of others and cheerfulness
in themselves. Some chapters of *L'Introduction à la vie dévote* read more like
guides for parenting than a handbook for religious meditation, as de Sales
counsels mothers that hygiene, recreation, and proper sleep are as necessary
as prayer for the Christian family.

The originality of the *Règlemens* lay in its incorporation of the simple virtues of domestic life into the convent and school life. The second book treats
the monastic community and echoes many of de Sales's recommendations.
Extreme ascetic practices, such as flagellation or prayer schedules that inter-
rupt sleep, were forbidden in the convent. All nuns received adequate food,
even on days of fasting. They were supplied with proper heating, clothing,
and comfortable beds. Every convent had its own infirmary, complete with
an apothecary for medical treatment. The daily routine included time for recreation—walks in the fresh air were highly encouraged—and private reflection. The *Règlemens* emphasizes the importance of good personal hygiene as
well as each nun's responsibility to keep both private quarters and communal
spaces, such as the dining refectory, clean. Only the mother superior could
punish offenses, and in those situations, she was encouraged to consider
the gravity of the fault, whether it was due to simple human weakness or
actual malice, before decreeing a punishment. The nuns were directed to
make mealtimes pleasant by exhibiting good manners and avoiding gossip,
disagreements, or special friendships that might lead to factions in the congregation. These rules had the goal of transforming the convent into a well-regu-
lated and pleasant home, where prayer and work were integrated and equally
valued. Like Merici's *Rule*, the *Règlemens* tacitly presents a simple method of
teacher training: the nuns were to model in their daily lives the good conduct
of pious women for their pupils to emulate.

In her comparative study of the Jesuit *Ratio studiorum* and the *Règlemens*,
St. Jean Martin makes a strong case for believing that the Ursulines of the first
house in Paris had received their teaching method from the Jesuits. Françoise
de Bermond had already sought the counsel of the Jesuits in Avignon about

34. François de Sales, *Introduction à la vie dévote* (Paris: Nelson, Editeurs, n.d.), 2.

effective ways to teach Catholic doctrine to children. Mme de Sainte-Beuve, the patron who called Bermond to Paris, received the idea of founding schools for girls from the Jesuit master of novices of Paris. Jesuits supported the Parisian Ursulines in the request they addressed to the Vatican to become a religious order, and three Jesuits helped prepare the 1640 constitutions. Given this collaboration, it is not an exaggeration to claim, as St. Jean Martin does, that "the *Règlements* were for the Ursulines what the *Ratio Studiorum* was for the Jesuits."[35]

We see the Jesuit influence in the organization of both pupils and faculty in the Ursuline schools. Like the *Ratio*, the *Règlemens* requires an administrative hierarchy that ensures the use of a common curriculum and teaching methods. Both documents give "common sets of regulations and specific prescriptions for the teachers of various subjects." In both the boys' and girls' schools, classes were formed of pupils of similar age and intellectual capacity.[36] These similarities demonstrate that, like the Jesuits, the Ursuline goal was to create a standardized educational system that could be used in any Ursuline convent school anywhere in France. In other ways, however, the educational system described in the *Règlemens* differed greatly from the Jesuit system. The early Jesuits did not have boarding schools because they wished to keep their devotional life distinct from their teaching duties, whereas the boarding school was the *raison d'être* of the Ursulines.[37] The Jesuit curriculum, based on the study of Greek and Latin languages and literatures, presupposed a mastery of reading and writing that was closer to secondary education than to the elementary education offered by the Ursulines. Moreover, the teaching methods approved in the *Ratio*, such as training in debate, did not meet the needs of girls, who were unlikely to engage in public philosophical argumentation. Given these important differences, it is more accurate to say that the Ursulines used the *Ratio studiorum* as a template rather than as a model to imitate.

THE EDUCATION OF GIRLS

The Ursulines of Paris had embarked on a complex project. The convent envisaged by Bermond and her patrons was to house two separate schools:

35. St. Jean Martin, *Ursuline Method*, 285, 289–91.
36. Ibid., 303, 307.
37. Eventually, circumstances required the Jesuits to form boarding schools. The first were in Germany and Portugal (St. Jean Martin, *Ursuline Method*, 316).

the more important boarding school for the daughters of the nobility and the bourgeoisie who would live year-round with the nuns, and a day school, where girls of working-class families could come for a few hours six days a week, if their family obligations permitted. The first book of *Les Règlemens des religieuses Ursulines de la Congrégation de Paris*, entitled "De ce qui concerne l'instruction des petites filles" (The Education of Girls), reflects this complexity. The book is divided into two parts, the first concerning the *pensionnat*, or boarding school, and the second dealing with the *externat*, or day school.

The boarders were to receive more than a simple preparation for the sacraments and basic instruction in reading, writing, arithmetic, and needlework. Under the guidance of the nuns and by their frequent attendance at mass and prayer services as well as their study of Christian doctrine, they would be introduced to the devout life and trained to become active Catholic wives and mothers. The *Règlemens* exhibits an effort to encourage personal devotion among the day pupils that was much more extensive than the sacramental preparation offered in the parish schools, where priests had taught reading and the rudiments of Christian doctrine to urban children in France since the Middle Ages. Moreover, if they were to realize the mission of their Italian founder, the French Ursulines needed a pedagogy that reenacted the mother-daughter relationship in their classrooms and a method flexible enough to be practiced in city and country, with girls of all social classes.

Seventeenth-century religious congregations were far from simple communities. All cloistered orders of the age, not only in France but throughout Catholic Europe, were composed of two categories of nuns: choir nuns, the daughters of the nobility or the wealthy middle class, whose obligations consisted of prayer, meditation, celebration of the liturgy, and teaching; and converse nuns, the daughters of workers or peasants, who also lived a life of prayer but, in addition, performed domestic functions and were not allowed to teach. Because choir nuns could not leave the convent, converse nuns acted as liaisons with the merchants and tradespeople of the outside world. Choir and converse nuns lived in separate quarters and occupied different areas of the church during mass and liturgical ceremonies. The typical convent also housed two novitiates, one for choir nuns and the other for converse nuns, and these novitiates were separated from each other and from the nuns who had already taken their vows.

Since the two student populations of the *pensionnat* and the *externat* did not mix, the Ursulines required two separate workforces. *Pensionnaires* needed their own dormitories, refectories, classrooms, and recreational spaces, all of which would be inside the convent and separated from the nuns' living spaces but nevertheless close enough to the nuns' quarters to benefit from their constant supervision. The *externes* (day pupils) would never cross paths with the boarders. Their classrooms, as well as the doors by which they came in and left, were not connected to the boarders' area, and they had their own teachers, administration, and helpers. The convent church—in some cases, no more than a chapel—was the only common ground of the community where nuns, boarders, and day students attended mass and received the sacraments. Chapter one of the first book acknowledges the complexity of the Ursuline enterprise and the need for a clear delineation of duties if the educational enterprise was to succeed:

Les Religieuses ursulines étant principalement établies pour s'employer à l'instruction et conduite des jeunes filles, et obligées par leurs constitutions de recevoir à ce sujet des pensionnaires dans leurs monastères, il est nécessaire pour qu'elles s'en puissent bien acquitter, et pour éviter le désordre et la confusion que la multitude de personnes et d'occupations a coutume d'apporter, que toutes choses soient bien ordonnées, et que les offices de celles qui y sont employées soient réglés en sorte que chacune, sans préjudicier à sa propre perfection, puissent procurer celles des filles qui lui sont commises.[38]

The Ursuline religious order has been founded principally for the instruction and upbringing of girls and is obliged by its constitutions to receive boarders into its monasteries. To carry out these obligations and to avoid the disorder and confusion that usually arise in a community made up of many people carrying out different tasks, it is necessary that everything be well organized and that the duties of the nuns charged with the education of boarders be established in regulations. These regulations will enable all nuns to bring about excellent results in the girls entrusted to them without harming their own spiritual lives.

38. *Les Règlemens des religieuses Ursulines de la Congrégation de Paris* (Paris: Chez Louis Josse, rue S. Jacques à la Couronne d'épines, 1705), book 1, pages 3–4. All further references will be from my English translation, cited parenthetically in the text by part, chapter, article (when there is one), and paragraph number. Readers interested in obtaining a digitized copy of the 1705 *Règlemens* will find it listed in the catalog of the Bibliothèque nationale de France as #8LD172-7.

ADMINISTRATION AND FACULTY

The administration of the boarding school consisted of a single person, the *maîtresse générale* (general mistress), who oversaw every part of student life and whose authority was second only to that of the mother superior of the convent. Her duties combined those of a modern director of studies with supervision of teachers. She inspected every classroom in the boarding school regularly, reviewing the performance of her teachers and their implementation of the curriculum. In addition, she was required to keep an eye on the girls during meals and to sleep near their dormitories, "pour être facilement avertie, s'il leur arrivait quelque besoin extraordinaire durant la nuit" (This will enable her to take care of any unexpected problem during the night [pt. 1, ch. 2, 27]). Her counterpart in the day school opened the doors to pupils each morning and decided when inclement weather justified late starts or early closings. The general mistress of each school was responsible for admissions, and she alone had the right to dismiss day students for absenteeism or tardiness. She regulated class size, disciplined pupils, and distributed rewards. Among her most demanding duties was the obligation to learn the family history and special circumstances of each pupil, a requirement in line with Merici's Mother Idea. This knowledge enabled the general mistress to assess the effectiveness of teachers as well as gauge student progress during her bimonthly visits to each classroom specified in the *Règlemens*. Finally, the *maîtresse générale* alone had the right and duty to interact with the parents or guardians of the boarders. The *Règlemens* calls upon her to meet from time to time with families and give an account of each girl's progress. In the case of the day school, the general mistress could receive written or oral messages from the parents explaining their daughter's attendance or requesting a leave of absence for the child.

Two *maîtresses de classe* (class mistresses) were assigned to each room in the boarding school to teach catechism and reading, the most important subjects of the curriculum. Although both mistresses taught, the older of the two, called the "first mistress," was charged with moral instruction and preparation for the sacraments. The *Règlemens* specifies that these mistresses take turns being *en semaine*, that is, acting as the lead teacher for a week. However, the mistress who was not en semaine was expected to be present for most of the school day to help the lead mistress with the chores of dressing and washing the boarders in the morning and bringing the girls to and from church services. She also supervised classwork during the lead teacher's breaks. When we read what was expected of these teachers—namely, to care for the boarders twenty-four hours every day, never leaving them alone even when they slept, supervising them during meals and recreation as well as in the classroom— we see the wisdom of supplying two teachers for a job that would quickly overwhelm a single one. While the rotation of duties described in the *Règle- mens* may seem rigid, there are passages that recognize the mistresses' right to respond to their own needs and those of their pupils with flexibility, in line with Angela Merici's tenet that teachers must be able to respond to changing times and circumstances. The section on supervising students on feast days, for example, states that nothing prevents the two mistresses from coming to their own agreement about substituting for each other (pt. 1, ch. 3, 13).

Three nuns handled the rest of the curriculum. They did not have class- rooms of their own and served the entire school. The *maîtresse de l'écriture* (writing mistress) taught pupils how to write words and sentences in legible script. She taught in the dining room, where each class came for an assigned period. The other two nuns went into the classroom and worked with smaller groups of pupils. "Celle qui enseigne le jet, la lecture en lettre de la main, et l'orthographe" (The one who teaches counting, reading handwritten texts, and spelling) was the most versatile teacher, as she was responsible for in- struction in arithmetic, teaching pupils how to understand letters and doc- uments written by hand, and, for the more advanced pupils, spelling. The *maîtresse des ouvrages* (needlework mistress) taught simple sewing as well as artistic stitchery, such as tapestry and embroidery (pt. 1, ch. 7, 3).

The faculty of the day school followed the model of the boarding school. There were two class mistresses and three specialized teachers. The *Règle- mens* states simply that the "écolières externes seront divisées en plusieurs classes selon la commodité du lieu, et le nombre des écolières" (day pupils will be divided into several classes whose size will be determined by the avail- ability of space and the number of pupils [pt. 2, ch. 1, 1]), a description that suggests the classes in the day school were normally much larger than those in the boarding school. The difficulty of providing adequate attention to day pupils resulted in one of the Ursulines' most important pedagogical innova- tions: the *dixainières*. These were older day pupils who helped the class mis- tress deal with large enrollments by overseeing a group of ten to twelve girls within the crowded classroom. More teacher aides than teaching assistants, their principal duties involved taking roll, maintaining order among the girls, monitoring behavior in class and during recreation, and distributing books and other supplies for classwork. Their only duty that approached actual teaching took place during catechism lessons, when they questioned pupils on their knowledge and understanding of dogma and helped them memorize catechism and prayers. *Dixainières* were nominated by the class mistresses but delegated by the general mistress for three- to four-month terms. It was an honor to become a *dixainière*, the recognition of good character, love of learning, and intelligence.

In addition to the administrator and teaching faculty, the boarding school had a *tourière* (gatekeeper), who interacted with the world outside the cloister, receiving and paying for food and school supplies, without leaving the convent. She also admitted visitors to the convent. The *Règlemens* devotes whole chapters to the *boursière* (bursar) and the *lingère* (linen mistress). The *boursière* was responsible for the school budget and was expected to keep up-to-date records of any cash and gifts coming into the schools. The *lingère* was responsible for the laundry of the nuns and boarders, a duty that involved mending and alterations as well as washing and maintaining inventories of clothing and linen. An *infirmière* (nurse) cared for all but the most serious illnesses of both boarders and nuns. The *tourière, boursière, lingère,* and *infirmière* were all choir nuns and were addressed, as were the teaching mistresses, by the title "mère" (mother). There was no need for such support staff in the day school, since the pupils did not live in the convent and went home for their midday meal. The general mistress took the place of the bursar, receiving the small sums wealthy pupils contributed.

The domestic duties in the boarding school were carried out by converse nuns who, because of their social status, did not have the right to teach. Although these nuns did perform some menial tasks, such as making the boarders' beds, the *Règlemens* makes it clear that all nuns, both choir and converse, were required to clean their own rooms and common rooms such as the dining hall, to serve meals, and to wash dishes. Once boarders were old enough, they, too, were expected to make their own beds and help sort, fold, and store laundry. Converse nuns were not so much servants as housekeepers vital to the success of the Ursuline mission. They could leave the convent on errands; they ran the kitchen, planted and tended the convent gardens, served as medical aides to the head nurse, and staffed the pharmacy. Because they did not teach, they were known as "soeurs" (sisters), rather than mères. This nominal distinction between teaching and nonteaching Ursuline nuns lasted until the 1970s, when the Second Vatican Council imposed the title of "sister" on all nuns.

Book 1 of the *Règlemens* does not address teacher training, but a chapter on the regulations governing novices included in the second book on monastic life makes it clear that the time spent in the novitiate prepared future choir nuns for the classroom as well as for the cloister. The chapter on regulations for the novices states that, under the direction of the *mère maîtresse* (mother mistress) and her assistants, the novices attended daily classes that stressed knowledge of the liturgy and the catechism. They were expected to read aloud in class as well as to spend several short periods every day in private reading of devotional texts, both in Latin and French. Instruction in subjects other than catechism and reading took place in the afternoon, when the novices worked on their skills in needlework, counting, and reading handwritten texts. While all choir novices were expected to teach catechism, reading, and needlework, a few were selected by the mother mistress to teach the more specialized subjects of arithmetic and reading handwritten letters.

Admission to the boarding school required an initial meeting between the general mistress and the family of the prospective student. Orphans could be admitted but only after the mother superior had consulted the adults who had legal custody of the girl, determined their good moral character, and received their approbation. If this meeting proved satisfactory, it was followed by the future pupil's visit to the school and interview with the mother superior. The meeting between parents or guardians and the general mistress served to acquaint the teachers with the family situation, special needs, and talents of each girl. It also provided the means of gaining the parents' assent to the requirements of life in a convent, which meant that the girl would not be allowed to go home on Sundays or feast days or even receive regular family visits during the entire course of her education. The visit by the girl, unaccompanied by her parents, gave her the opportunity to express enthusiasm or doubts before entering into a life that would involve not only learning to read and write but living alongside nuns and spending a good part of each day in prayer. The mother superior of the convent, who also exercised the highest authority in the schools, had the final say about admitting a girl. The paragraphs describing the interviews with parents and future pupils contain the phrases "s'il ne se trouve point d'empêchement" or "si . . . on ne trouve rien qui empêche" (pt. 1, ch. 2, 11, 12), which translate as "if there are no other obstacles." Such caveats suggest that the nuns retained the right to refuse any girl who had no interest in education or any parents who forced unwilling children into the school. The *Règlemens* makes it very clear that the boarding school was not intended as a recruitment center for future Ursuline nuns. The chapters on the general mistress and the class mistresses outline a complicated process for dealing with older boarders considering the religious life that included interviews with the mother superior, the general mistress, and teachers, requiring the girl to spend a year outside of the convent to confirm her vocation and, in the extreme case of a girl being deemed unfit, asking her parents to withdraw her from the school.

Admission to the day school was simpler and only required an interview between the general mistress and the pupil seeking admission. The pupil had to give evidence of her personal piety, as well as that of her family, but also to explain how her family duties would allow her to attend class. The *Règlemens* suggests that what today we would term a "background check" took place for each aspiring pupil to the day school: "Elle [the general mistress] n'en admettra aucune . . . qu'elle n'ait assurance par personnes connues que ses parents, ou ceux chez qui elle demeure, font de bonne vie" (She will not admit any girl . . . if she cannot be assured by someone well acquainted with the family that the parents or guardians are of good moral character [pt. 2, ch. 2,10]). Both interviews and investigations into the familial circumstances of each student gave the nuns the ability to control admissions. The day school's requirement that a pupil not only know the letters of the alphabet but also know how to assemble the letters into simple words, "sache les assembler" (pt. 2, ch. 2, 9), ensured that girls entered class prepared to learn.

Neither the boarding nor the day school charged any fee for instruction. However, families of boarders were expected to furnish their girls with modest, simple clothing and pay the costs of their room and board. Families of day students who had the means to do so were asked to contribute wood for heating as well as small sums for the purchase of class supplies, such as paper and ink. The *Règlemens* indicates that the Ursulines took great care to avoid any appearance of misusing funds. The bursar kept a careful record of all money coming in, and the general mistress alone could authorize the distribution of any gifts of money from the boarders' families. It was strictly forbidden for a class mistress to ask pupils for money, "non pas même pour l'employer en aumône" (even if she intended to give it in alms to the poor [pt. 1, ch. 3, 33]). The general mistress of the day school could not make a profit from any books the pupils had paid her to purchase for their use. Gifts of money from families went to the classroom of the contributing family's daughter and could be used only for the embellishment of class oratories or for end-of-year awards.

COMPOSITION OF CLASSES
IN THE BOARDING AND DAY SCHOOLS

The *Règlemens* respected the social distinctions of old regime France. The boarding school was restricted to girls of the ancient noble families as well as the newly ennobled legal and merchant classes. The day school not only kept the pupils of lower-class families apart from the boarders but also separated day students of better-off families from those who were indigent. The *Règlemens* directs the day-school teachers to "prendr[e] garde de ne pas mettre les filles de condition proche des plus pauvres et malpropres pour ne leur point donner de dégoût" (take care not to place pupils from wealthier families too close to the ones who are poor and dirty, lest the wealthier pupils find the poorer ones distasteful [pt. 2, ch. 3, 22]). No girl, however, was refused an education because of her social class or wealth. The same paragraph that mandates the separation of rich and poor into different spaces in the classroom continues with the admonition that teachers minimize the effects of such distinctions, separating the girls "avec discrétion: afin que les pauvres ne se croient pas méprisées, et elles marqueront en tout, aux unes et aux autres, un égal soin et une égale affection, sans aucune acceptation des personnes" (with discretion, lest the poor girls feel they are being scorned. At all times the class mistresses will show the same respect and affection to all pupils, without regard to a pupil's condition [pt. 2, ch. 3, 22]). If poor girls chose to work in the day school—for example, as custodians—they were not treated as servants but, rather, received payment for their work and never performed chores, such as cleaning the classroom, in the presence of other pupils. The Ursulines justified such equal treatment by invoking the gospel mandate to imitate Christ, a fitting injunction for teachers whose principal goal was the formation of devout wives and mothers: "Les Religieuses qui sont destinées à l'instruction des écolières externes s'y doivent porter avec d'autant plus d'affection, qu'en cette occupation elles imitent de plus près le Fils de Dieu: lequel pendant sa vie a voulu principalement instruire les pauvres et les ignorans" (The nuns who have been chosen to teach day pupils should carry out their work lovingly, all the more so because this work allows them to imitate more closely the Son of God, whose central mission, during His time on earth, was to teach the poor and ignorant [pt. 2, ch. 3, 1]).

The *Constitutions* of 1640 stated that only girls between the ages of six and fifteen could be admitted to the school.[39] However, nowhere is a specific age for incoming pupils given in the *Règlemens*, except for the mention that girls over eighteen were too old to enter the *pensionnat* and that the day school only accepted older teenagers for sacramental preparation. Several passages suggest that boarders began instruction later than our contemporary elementary school children. Since boarders did not go home for vacation or holidays and only spent the night away from the convent on rare occasions, such as when they became seriously ill or a family member died, they had to be old enough to understand that they would be separated from their parents and assent to life in the convent. They had to accept the responsibilities of prayer and serious study explained in the "Regulations for Boarders." These requirements suggest that girls might have been no younger than nine or ten when they entered the boarding school and that many were already teenagers. Once accepted, girls were organized into classes according to "âge et capacité"—age and ability—with "ability" understood as a function of age. The Ursulines did not make exceptions for what we would call today "gifted" or "special needs" children. Girls whose physical condition could not withstand the fatigue and effort of study were not admitted. This system of grouping pupils according to age made sense in the boarding school because these girls lived and studied together year-round, and great differences in age in a single class might have made communal living more difficult for the girls and more complicated for the nuns who looked after them. An age-based system also helped with the placement of incoming girls. Since the seventeenth-century schools did not have the modern notion of an academic year, with beginning and ending dates, girls entered the boarding school at different times of the year, and it was far easier to determine their age than their level of competence in any academic subject.

In the day school, classes were also composed of pupils of similar age, again because of the notion that children of similar age had similar intellectual capacities and maturity. Day pupils had to know the alphabet, as well as the spelling of simple words, before entering the school, a requirement that suggests they could have been as young as today's first graders. The only exceptions were older girls wishing to receive the sacraments, who could be completely illiterate and who only studied catechism. Day pupils waited

39. *Constitutions*, part 1, 31.

until the beginning of the month to begin instruction, when they were placed, again according to age, in a class already in session. In an effort to limit class size, those girls in each class who had proved more able could be moved into a class of older pupils or could serve as *dixainières*, thus allowing teachers more time for individual instruction of the newer or slower pupils. The *Règlemens* makes no mention of how long a girl could remain in the day school. The duration of her studies depended on her commitment to regular attendance, the desires of her parents, and her need to work but also on the assent of the religious community. Many girls probably left once they had completed their religious instruction, but no regulations or financial problems would have prevented them from remaining in school until late adolescence.

The matter of when girls entered and left the Ursuline convent points to important differences between the early Ursuline concept of school and our modern one. We have seen that these educators had no notion of an academic year. They did not give letter or number grades to distinguish the better pupils from the poorer ones. All girls in a class did not celebrate their First Communion in the same year but only those who were deemed sufficiently mature to receive the sacrament, while others in the class did so in a later year. There were no diplomas signifying the successful completion of a curriculum. Preparation to receive the sacraments, most importantly the Eucharist, was the primary goal of the Ursuline education. Certainly, girls who spent several years in the boarding school improved their reading, writing, and computational skills because they had many hours of practice, but they did not advance from basic to more sophisticated studies, such as from arithmetic to algebra. They were taught from the moment they entered either the boarding or the day school that their principal duty was to grow in understanding of Catholic doctrine, as well as in virtue and devotion. The school day and calendar were ordered to promote this spiritual progress.

DAILY SCHEDULE

Chapter eight of the first part, "De l'ordre que les pensionnaires doivent garder" (Schedules the Boarders Will Observe), describes the way in which devotional exercises punctuated the school day. Boarders rose at 5:30 or 6:00 a.m., said their morning prayers, and attended mass before breakfast. At the end of the two hours of morning classes, they said the Litanies of the Virgin and then ate their midday meal listening to readings from Scripture, the lives of the saints, or the histories of Jesuit missionaries. Having said grace after meals, they went to recess. The two hours of afternoon class concluded with vespers. The study of catechism for a full hour ended the school day. After supper, boarders said parts of the Liturgy of the Hours, then examined their conscience and went to bed.

The *Règlemens* demonstrates a sincere effort to help day pupils carry out a life of prayer similar to that of the boarders. Upon entering the school, girls were immediately helped by their *dixainières* to learn the prayers they would say daily in their homes upon waking, taking their meals, and before sleeping as well as those they would say before the beginning of each class period in the school. The nuns taught them to make an examination of conscience when they went to bed. Day pupils, like boarders, went to confession in the convent chapel once a month and received communion upon request to the class mistress and approval by the general mistress. The school prepared them for Confirmation, a sacrament they received in their parish church rather than in the convent church. When a day pupil left the school, she had a final meeting, during which the first class mistress spoke to her in private, "pour lui recommender de vivre chrétiennement et [de] penser aux choses plus nécessaires à son salut" (urging her to live a good Christian life and always to think about what she must do to gain eternity [pt. 2, ch. 3, 19]) and thus carry her Ursuline education into her family life to guide her future comportment.

The classrooms and school calendars in both schools were set up to encourage devotional practices. Every classroom had an oratory that the girls decorated. It could be as simple as a single religious painting or as elaborate as an armoire furnished with a table, statues, and other images. Half-days and full holidays occurred frequently as the school followed the rhythm of the liturgical year. Boarders participated fully in liturgical celebrations, especially during Lent and Easter, such as Palm Sunday processions. In addition, each class in both schools had opportunities to hold more personal celebrations. On the feast day of either the class patron or their own patron saint, boarders could invite anyone in the school who venerated that saint to hear the class sing litanies and hymns. In the day school, the choice of a monthly class patron involved drawing the name of a saint from a vessel. If the feast day of the chosen patron saint fell within that month, the day pupils, too, could celebrate the occasion by singing and inviting other classes to the ceremony. Certainly, the most important celebration in the life of a boarder or day pupil in the Ursuline schools was her First Communion. The girls chosen from each class enjoyed six or seven weeks of special attention from their class mistress or the general mistress of the school and then received the congratulations and blessings of the entire school when they received the Eucharist for the first time. The importance given to sacramental preparation in Ursuline schools marked a milestone in a girl's devotional life that was duly celebrated.

THE MOTHER IDEA

The opening paragraph of the *Règlemens* simply states that the Ursuline order was established "pour s'employer à l'instruction et conduite des jeunes filles" (for the instruction and upbringing of girls [pt. 1, ch. 1, 1]). By the use of the term *conduite*, which here signifies guidance or the formation of character and behavior, the nuns acknowledged their obligation not simply to impart knowledge but also to take charge of the pupil's upbringing. Using the mother-daughter relationship as their model, they developed a pedagogy that took into account the physical and spiritual, as well as intellectual, needs of each girl. The *Règlemens* reveals an almost obsessive concern with the boarders' physical well-being. The general mistress was required to take great care of those who fell sick, sending them back to their parents in the case of serious illness. The boarders' living quarters, as well as their classrooms, were heated throughout the winter, and girls dressed warmly. At table, the general mistress ensured that meals were made with quality ingredients and served in generous portions. The boarders ate four times a day: breakfast, the main meal at midday, an afternoon snack, and evening supper.

Chapters eleven and twelve of the first part, concerning the rules for those nuns charged with dressing the boarders and supervising their beds, address more than once the importance of instilling habits of personal cleanliness, especially of the hair, hands, and teeth. The chapters on the day pupils make little mention of hygiene or food because these girls came to school already dressed and went home for meals. The chapter on the daily schedule, however, permits girls who have not eaten at home to eat breakfast in the assembly area where they wait to enter the school in the morning and even to eat during class time, both in the morning and afternoon, if they have permission to do so. The general mistress of the *écolières externes* provided wood to heat the classrooms in the winter, and she adjusted the start and end of the school days according to the seasons and weather conditions, allowing girls to arrive later and leave earlier in the winter—"afin qu'elles puissent s'en retourner plus commodément chez elles" (she will allow the pupils to leave earlier so they can get home more safely [pt. 2, ch. 2, 7]). Although all girls were supposed to come into school at the same time every morning, the *Règlemens* recognized that this was not always possible and permitted the general mistress to open the door a second time for late-comers, "pour obvier aux inconvénients qui pourraient arriver, si elles demeuraient vagabondes tout ce temps-là (to ward off any problems that could arise if the girls wandered about unsupervised for a long time [pt. 2, ch. 2, 6]). The day pupils, as well as the boarders, benefited from the nuns' constant supervision.

The *Règlemens* recognized the importance of a good night's rest. Girls went to bed at 8:00 p.m. and didn't waken until 5:30 or 6:00 a.m., and somewhat later in the winter, which meant they had nine or ten hours of sleep every night. Both boarders and day pupils were encouraged to develop strategies that would help them allay nighttime fears or difficulties in falling asleep. As the final lines of the regulations for boarders recommend: "Avant de se coucher, elles adoreront Dieu, . . . [et] prendront de l'eau bénite; et, ayant donné le bonsoir à leur maîtresse, elles se coucheront modestement, essayant de s'endormir sur quelque bonne pensée (Before they get into bed, they will adore God . . . , make the sign of the cross with holy water, and, having wished their mistress good night, get in bed without making a fuss and try to think good thoughts as they fall asleep [pt. 1, ch. 15, 37]). The regulations for day pupils include a similar recommendation that girls "give their hearts to God as they did in the morning and try to fall asleep while thinking good thoughts."

Recreation was also important. Boarders had two recesses, each lasting between forty-five minutes and an hour. The first, following the midday meal, was supervised by the class mistress, who led the girls in simple games. This paragraph does not specify what counted as appropriate games, only prohibiting "comédies, danses, cartes et autres semblables" (acting, dancing, playing card games, or other such things [pt. 1, ch. 3, 28]). Given that the nuns themselves were encouraged to get physical exercise and that the hours of evening recess were extended in the summer to take advantage of sunlight and good weather, we can assume that the "simple games" included physical activities, at least strolls around the convent grounds. Boarders used the second recess, which followed the evening meal and preceded bedtime, in quieter occupations, such as reading or handwork, and could even prepare themselves for bed earlier if they preferred to do so. The day pupils had no regular recess during their shortened school day, but like the boarders, they enjoyed frequent holidays on feast days. Saturday afternoons and Sundays they had no classes.

As girls matured and moved from the lower- to the higher-level classes, the nuns expected pupils to take more care of themselves and participate in the domestic tasks of the community, much as the mother of a large family might do with an older daughter. While the nuns did everything for the youngest boarders, from dressing them to helping them individually, the older boarders not only took care of themselves but also assisted the *lingère* with folding laundry, mending clothing, ironing, and setting and clearing the table at meals. In the day school, girls took turns leading the class in prayers, sweeping the classroom floor at the end of the school day, and serving as *dixainières*. Thus, during their years with the Ursulines, both groups of pupils learned to work with their classmates and to assume responsibility for themselves and their community—useful assets for girls destined to become wives and mothers.

The Ursulines strictly forbade physical punishments, such as whipping and withholding food or heat that might endanger the health of the boarders. They also prevented any sudden angry reactions from the class mistresses by giving the authority for discipline uniquely to the general mistress. In the day school, the only offense meriting expulsion was absenteeism. Otherwise, "light faults," such as making noise, not studying, or being rude to classmates, were first handled by a private remonstrance from the teacher. If this failed, the teacher imposed "une petite confusion devant toutes, comme de les mettre les dernières de leur banc, ou en une place à part, les faire tenir quelque temps debout" (the mistress should cause the pupil some slight embarrassment, like making her sit at the back of the class or away from the other pupils or stand for a short time, etc. [pt. 2, ch. 3, 25]). The nuns were not naive; in fact, the *Règlemens* recognizes that some girls will be compliant and diligent in their studies while others will be lazy and have bad dispositions. The remedy, however, lay in treating bad behavior with "une grande charité" (great charity) that made light of small offenses.

The routine of the school day provided an additional means of modeling behavior. The *Règlemens* specified the amount of time dedicated to every activity and often the hours and minutes when activities began and ended. The purpose of such a detailed timetable was, in part, to speak to the concerns of earlier Christian writers on girls' education. Already in the sixteenth century, Erasmus of Rotterdam had praised study as a way to protect girls from the dangers of idleness.[40] Similarly, Fénelon feared that a girl with too much time on her hands would easily succumb to the temptations of harmful activities such as gossip and love of fashion. He cautioned mothers to keep their daughters close by their side,[41] not only directing their studies but capitalizing on every experience of the day to learn about household management, hygiene, and nature. The packed schedule established in the *Règlemens*, coupled with the personal attention pupils received in and out of the classroom, left little opportunity for objectionable behavior.

We find the most obvious proof of the respect the Ursulines accorded to their pupils in the lengthy chapter entitled *"Règlemens pour les pensionnaires"* (Regulations for the Boarders). There is no mention of punishments but, rather, elucidation of the girls' duties toward God, themselves, and their parents. These duties included daily prayer, hygiene, kindness toward their fellow pupils, and obedience as well as gratitude to their real parents and to the surrogate mothers caring for them in the convent. The boarders were reminded of this rule at least once during every school year, when it was read to them either by the class mistress or the general mistress in assembly. A much briefer *"Règlemens pour les externes"* (Regulations for Day Pupils) requires even these girls who spent but a few hours in the convent to develop piety through morning and evening prayer and frequent reception of the sacraments, to respect and obey their teachers and *dixainières*, and to treat their classmates with respect and to avoid frivolous behavior outside of school and within.

CURRICULUM AND TEACHING METHODS

The curriculum described in the *Règlemens* was a basic elementary course of study that consisted of seven subjects: catechism, reading, writing, counting and arithmetic, needlework, reading handwritten texts, and spelling. The boarding school offered between four and five hours of instruction on a full day of school and two hours on half-days; the day school had four hours on a full day and two on half-days. Of the seven subjects, the most important were reading, which was taught both morning and afternoon for forty-five minutes, and catechism, taught for forty-five minutes at the end of the school day. Needlework was the only other class held twice a day, in the morning and afternoon, although for shorter periods of time than reading. Writing class,

40. Sowards, "Erasmus and the Education of Women," 83.
41. Fénelon, *De l'Education des filles*, chapters 9, 11.

like reading, also lasted forty-five minutes. Arithmetic, spelling, and hand-written texts took up the rest of the school day. Even on half-days, some time was spent on arithmetic, needlework, catechism, and reading. Writing could be skipped on half-days because it required a good deal of time to prepare the room and the writing materials for each group of pupils. Boarders in the lower classes concentrated on reading and were deemed too young to study handwritten texts and spelling. In the day school, instruction in arithmetic, needlework, spelling, and reading handwritten texts was not always possible if there were too many pupils and not enough teachers; however, every class in the day school had two class mistresses, and at least one writing mistress served the entire school.

The chapter on the regulations for the class mistresses gives two methods for teaching reading. Both methods required that each girl have her own copy of the same book as that used by the mistress.[42] In the first method, the mistress sat among the pupils and had them read some portion of the day's lesson one after another. In the second, the mistress stood in front of the class and read aloud four or five lines from the book, pronouncing each word slowly and distinctly. She then read one or two full pages, this time insisting upon the proper intonation of the passage through the rise and fall of her voice and pauses made at the end of clauses and sentences. As the mistress read, the pupils followed the lesson in their books, imitating the mistress's pronuncia-tion and intonation in a low voice. This initial reading finished, the mistress required each girl to reread a part of the lesson aloud until the entire lesson had been repeated and any pronunciation mistakes corrected. In both the boarding school and the day school, reading was taught first in Latin, then in French, with Latin considered the easier language because the spelling corresponded so closely to the pronunciation. The goal of both methods was to enable readers to connect the printed word and the spoken word and to recognize, through extensive practice, the spoken word in the written word. Unlike the curriculum in Jesuit schools, in which Latin grammar, rhetoric, and literature were studied seriously and constituted a major part of the cur-riculum, in the Ursuline schools, Latin simply provided an entryway into reading French.[43]

42. Chervel tells us that these books probably contained religious writings (*Histoire*, 5). We do not have copies of any of these books, which may have been composed by the Ursulines themselves.

43. André Chervel's monumental history of the teaching of the French language gives us an idea of the problems confronting teachers of French in the seventeenth century. Millions of people living

In seventeenth-century schools, writing was the third step in literacy, and pupils only learned to write once they could read in Latin and had mastered reading in French. Writing, done only in French, was closer to the fine art of calligraphy than to the practical skill of communication.[44] The *Règlemens* adheres to this conception. The writing mistress started by showing girls how to hold a pen correctly, to apply ink neatly to paper, and to avoid smearing or blotting ink on paper. Good posture was so important that girls who did not sit straight were not allowed to write as much as those who did so. Girls learned to form individual letters, first the vowels and consonants whose strokes were of the same height, then consonants with longer upstrokes or downstrokes, before proceeding to the formation of complete words, then lines of words, then sentences in which the correct spacing between letters and words was respected.[45] Most of writing class involved practice, during which time the mistress circulated among her pupils, correcting mistakes and even holding and guiding any unsteady hands. For the more advanced pupils, she provided examples of good penmanship in the form of maxims of pious sayings that they could imitate. The most advanced pupils had permission to show off their skills in letters they wrote to their parents, which the writing mistress corrected.

Once eight or ten pupils from a class had developed "la main suffisamment affermie" (mastery of handwriting [pt. 1, ch. 6, 11]), they learned to spell from the same mistress who taught arithmetic and the reading of handwritten letters. She held spelling class for the boarders during the study period preceding catechism. The *Règlemens* gives two methods for teaching spelling, both of which involve the traditional French spelling test, the *dictée* (dictation), and memorization through practice. In the first, the mistress read several lines

---

on French soil could not speak the language much less read it. There was no formal study of French grammar. Then, as now, French spelling presented the exceptional problem of not corresponding to pronunciation (ibid., 83). According to Chervel, the Ursuline "oral method" was highly efficacious and was a major step forward in the teaching of the French language, one that made the study of spelling possible and would eventually lead to the study of grammar, literature, and composition: "Dès le début du XVIIe siècle, chez les ursulines par exemple, elles [les filles] apprennent l'orthographe, la grammaire, la littérature française, la poésie, l'art de rédiger les lettres. L'enseignement du français doit beaucoup aux institutions des demoiselles, où il a pris son essor" (ibid., 43).

44. Ibid., 140.

45. In my email correspondence with Yves Charles Morin of the University of Montreal (May 8, 2020), I learned that this sequence of letter formation was used commonly in the seventeenth century by "maîtres d'écrire," specialists in teaching writing.

from a spelling manual, pronouncing each word slowly and distinctly as the pupils wrote the words on paper. She then distributed the manuals to the pupils, who wrote the proper form of any words they had misspelled above the mistake. Without looking at their original work, the pupils wrote the text a second time and continued to write the same text on the following days until they no longer made mistakes. In the second method, after the mistress dictated the text, individual pupils spelled each word aloud, with the mistress correcting any mistakes, and the rest of the group wrote the proper form of the word above any misspellings. As with the first method, the pupils then rewrote the text until they did so perfectly. Rather than approaching spelling through grammar rules or vocabulary lists, these methods relied upon coordinating the hand and the ear through repetition so that the pupil could visualize what she heard and then re-create the proper spelling on paper.

The *Règlemens* refers to arithmetic with the term *jeter* because small objects called *jetons* (counters) were used in instruction. Girls learned to count in both Roman and Arabic numerals, both of which commonly appeared in books and commerce. They mastered addition, subtraction, and multiplication through repeated counting exercises, and when they were able to write numbers, they did sums on paper. They performed word problems that applied their understanding of arithmetic to everyday situations, such as figuring out the cost of a measure of cloth. The paragraphs on arithmetic specify that girls should also learn to pay in "diverses sortes de monnaie" (several denominations of coins [pt. 1, ch. 8, 3]), as both gold and silver currency were used in business transactions. Girls spent the majority of their time practicing arithmetic until they could calculate quickly.

Historian Shirley Kersey points out that embroidery, beginning in the Middle Ages, was "more scholarly than frivolous. Patterns of geometrical designs, allegories, Biblical stories, and Greek mythology demanded knowledge of history and literature, theology and design, color mixing and needlework techniques."[46] Parents sending their daughters to board with the Ursulines in the late seventeenth and eighteenth centuries would have considered needlework a necessary element of their education. The *Règlemens* acknowledges this importance in the chapter on the duties of the needlework mistress, stating that, in addition to knowing a variety of complicated stitches used in both French and English artistic needlework, she should be prepared to

46. "Medieval Education of Girls and Women," *Horizons* 58, no. 4 (Summer 1980): 188.

teach "autres ouvrages qui sont en usage dans le pays, et que leurs parents souhaitent qu'elles sachent" (any other types of needlework commonly done in the school's region or that the parents of the boarders wish their daughters to learn [pt. 1, ch. 7, 3]). Learning needlework also involved an understanding of the tools used—in this case, the different types of cloth and needles—as well as the care of these tools. As with spelling and writing, girls moved from simpler tasks, such as knotting thread, darning, and sewing hems, to embroidery and tapestry; they could not progress until they had mastered the simpler tasks. The needlework mistress spent a good deal of class time demonstrating not only how to form stitches but how to correct poorly made stitches, even guiding the pupil's hand, if necessary. Her workload was such that, like the writing mistress, she had the right to a daily assistant who practiced stitches with groups of two or three girls at a time while the mistress gave the primary instruction. The day school only benefited from a needlework mistress if there were enough teaching nuns to cover all the other subjects.

The ability to read handwritten texts such as letters, contracts, and other legal documents was a valuable skill that allowed a girl to understand business transactions and carry on a correspondence without the aid of an amanuensis. The *Règlemens* treats this subject very briefly in the same chapter as spelling and arithmetic. Instead of books, the mistress used actual handwritten documents that pupils deciphered on their own, trying to recognize letters they had already learned to form and to understand the meaning of abbreviations. If the class was large, it was divided into two groups so that each pupil could receive more attention from the mistress.

CATECHISM

Twenty-first-century Catholics may be surprised to learn that the catechism classes required of all children preparing to receive the sacraments of Confession, Communion, and Confirmation had their origin in the Counter-Reformation. The Council of Trent had produced a Roman Catechism in 1566 for the use of the clergy, but the need for summaries of Christian doctrine that taught basic truths of the faith to the laity were first imagined by the Protestant reformers Martin Luther and John Calvin.[47] Karen E. Carter pin-

47. Luther's *Small Catechism* for the instruction of children was published in 1529; Calvin's *Geneva Catechism*, in 1560.

points the appearance of Catholic versions in France as having occurred in
the final decades of the seventeenth century, when bishops from throughout
the country produced catechisms intended specifically for the instruction of
children.[48] A further impetus to the composition of diocesan catechisms was
the need to standardize religious education in the effort to combat Protestantism. Although published in many different parts of France, these catechisms
all treated the same fundamental articles of faith and the significance of the
sacraments. Subjects studied included the Apostles' Creed; the theological
virtues of faith, hope, and charity; the Ten Commandments; the "four ends of
man" (death, judgment, paradise, hell); as well as more specifically Catholic
doctrines, such as the Communion of Saints and the Transubstantiation.[49]
Doctrine was approached through what Carter terms "ritualized communication with God," that is, prayer, especially the Our Father and the Hail
Mary.[50] Catechisms most often appeared in the form of questions and answers, which children were expected to memorize, but also to understand and
believe, before they were deemed ready to receive the sacraments. In addition
to sacramental preparation, "the purpose of catechism was to teach God's
eternal truths and to encourage people to live their lives in harmony with these
truths."[51] This emphasis on children's education as the best means of forming
a future generation of Catholic adults is no different from the purpose of an
Ursuline education expressed in the opening lines of the 1705 Règlemens,
except for the one striking difference that it was nuns, not priests, who took
charge of this religious education.

Catechism is treated in chapter four, "De la Manière dont les maîtresses
doivent instruire les pensionnaires aux choses de piété" (How the Mistresses
Must Instruct the Boarders in Piety). The initial paragraphs describe the class
schedule. Each forty-five-minute lesson was divided into three fifteen-minute
segments. For the initial fifteen minutes, in the boarding school, one pupil,
previously chosen by the mistress, read the day's catechism and then questioned her classmates one at a time on the content of the reading. The goal

48. Karen E. Carter, "The Science of Salvation: French Diocesan Catechisms and Catholic Reform (1650–1800)," *Catholic Historical Review* 96, no. 2 (April 2010): 234–61. Carter found that
between 1650 and 1700, French bishops throughout France published at least 57 catechisms and that
the number of catechisms published had grown to 181 by 1800 (241).
49. Ibid., 244.
50. Ibid., 245.
51. Ibid., 252.

of these questions was to determine what the others had retained and understood from her reading. In the day school, the *dixainières* performed this duty. The second fifteen minutes engaged in a review of the previous day's material. This review was conducted by the class mistress through questions and answers that assessed not only how well the pupils had memorized the catechism but also their comprehension of Catholic dogma. If the mistress judged that the pupils had understood very little, she repeated the previous lesson until she was satisfied with their grasp of the subject matter. Pupils were encouraged to ask the mistress questions pertinent to the subject.

Mistresses spent the final fifteen minutes on the catechism lesson introduced at the beginning of class and explained doctrine in terms the children could grasp. The *Règlemens* suggests the use of stories, such as episodes from the life of Christ, to teach younger boarders who were not familiar with the New Testament. For more complicated subjects, such as the theological virtues or the sacraments, "on se servira de comparaisons familières, et conformes à leurs capacités" (the mistress should use comparisons with familiar things the boarders are capable of understanding [pt. i, ch. 4, art. i, 4]).[52] Although the *Règlemens* urged mistresses to prepare catechism lessons carefully and suggested the Roman Catechism (that is, the Catechism of the Council of Trent), the pedagogical works of Cardinal Richelieu, and the theological treatises of the Italian Jesuit, Robert Bellarmine, as references, the mistresses were warned not to repeat what they found in these books word for word but, rather, to take from these texts "seulement ce qui pourra les accommoder, selon la capacité de leurs pensionnaires" (only what they find helpful and what the boarders are capable of understanding [pt. i, ch. 4, art. i, 9]). Catechism lesson ended with the mistress exhorting pupils to apply what they had learned in the day's lesson to their own lives and to increase their love of God and determination to be virtuous:

Comme si l'on parlait de la création, les exciter à remercier Dieu de les avoir créées pour une fin si noble: et de leur avoir donné une âme capable de L'aimer, et de jouir éternellement de Lui. Si l'on parle des mystères de notre Rédemption, les porter à l'amour de notre Seigneur

52. The *Règlemens* does not give examples of such comparisons, but we can imagine they might include Saint Patrick's well-known comparison between the three leaves of the shamrock and the Trinity.

Jésus-Christ; et leur apprendre, principalement aux plus grandes, à faire des actes de Foy, d'Espérance, et de Charité." (pt. I, ch. 4, art. i, 5)

If the subject is the Creation, she should encourage them to thank God for having made them for such a noble purpose and for having given them a soul capable of loving Him and enjoying eternal happiness with Him. If they are talking about the mystery of the Redemption, she should incite them to love our Savior Jesus Christ and teach them, especially the older boarders, how to make acts of Faith, Hope, and Charity.

The special care taken to make catechism meaningful reflects the Ursuline mission to serve girls of all ages and intellectual maturity. Although the different subjects that composed the school day required different teaching techniques—repetition for writing, spelling, and needlework; memorization for reading, spelling, and catechism; analysis for arithmetic, deciphering handwriting, and catechism—similar principles guided the teachers in every interaction with their pupils. The first of these was to pay sufficient attention to every pupil, those who learned quickly and those who did not. The second was to consider teaching a vocation for both mistress and pupil. Every chapter on the duties of the teaching mistresses contains a paragraph urging the nuns to devote each minute of class time to instruction and to avoid frivolous conversation or activities. Similarly, the *Règlemens* impresses upon both boarders and day pupils their debt to their parents and teachers for the privilege of an education as well as their duty to make the most of their time in school. This seriousness of purpose that the French Ursulines extended to their pupils accounts in no small measure for the success of their educational enterprise in the seventeenth and eighteenth centuries.

TWO

A

Comparison

OF THE 1705 AND 1860

Regulations

THE HISTORY OF EDUCATION IN NINETEENTH-CENTURY FRANCE is as complicated as the history of the country's ever-changing central government, from the First Republic (1792–1804) to the First Empire (1804–1814) to the Bourbon and Orléans monarchies (1815–1848), Second Republic (1848–1851), Second Empire (1851–1870), and, finally, Third Republic (1871–1940). All the problems that arose with attempts to create a national education system—whether they concerned central versus local control, elementary versus secondary instruction, separate-sex versus mixed-sex schools, teacher training, or financing—were also entangled with the conflicts between the Catholic Church and anti-clerical forces. As Raymond Grew and Patrick Harrigan observe, "Over any number of issues and at any level of French life, skirmishes could take place; but even at their bitterest, during the Third Republic, the most common battlefield was education."[1]

Before the French Revolution, for all but the noble and wealthy who employed tutors, elementary education was in the hands of the Catholic Church. From the time of Louis XIV, priests ran *écoles paroissales* (parish schools), where they or male lay teachers instructed children of both sexes in catechism

1. Raymond Grew and Patrick Harrigan, "The Catholic Contribution to Universal Schooling in France, 1850–1906," *Journal of Modern History* 57 (June 1985): 211–47.

51

and reading. Girls of the nobility and bourgeoisie boarded in convents, where cloistered nuns prepared them for the sacraments and taught them reading, writing, and stitchery. With the advent of the Ursulines, daughters of the poor or lower classes could attend convent day schools. One of the main goals of the French Revolution was to eradicate the influence of the Catholic Church in all aspects of French life. It effectively did so in the sphere of education when it confiscated church property, closed convents and monasteries, and persecuted male and female religious during the Reign of Terror (1793). If the Revolution succeeded in destroying the monopoly of the church in education, it did not get around to putting anything in its place.[2]

Napoleon did much to solve this problem with the Concordat of 1801 between France and the Vatican. Among other conflicts it resolved between the French Crown and Rome, the Concordat allowed the traditional French Catholic teaching orders—the Christian Brothers and Jesuits for boys and the Ursulines for girls—to rebuild their schools. Beginning in the first years of the century, French society was also marked by the creation of over four hundred congregations of women motivated by piety but also by a desire to care for the poor and serve as teachers. Claude Langlois has studied this phenomenon, which he terms "Le Catholicisme au féminin" (Catholicism in the feminine), which resulted in priests taking a back seat to nuns in the public sphere.[3] Rebecca Rogers offers several explanations for the appeal of religious life to pious women. Most significant, the convent was an important alternative to family life; "it represented a degree of autonomy and independence as well as the latitude to engage in public life in ways few secular women found possible."[4] No longer obliged as the Ursulines had been in the seventeenth century to live in cloister, these women interacted with the secular world and were sometimes encouraged by the emperor to establish schools, especially in the cities.[5] As Ann Margaret Doyle explains, this arrangement was to Napoleon's

2. Ann Margaret Doyle, "Catholic Church and State Relations in French Education in the Nineteenth Century: The Struggle between *Laïcité* and Religion," *International Studies in Catholic Education* 9, no. 1 (March 2017): 110.

3. Claude Langlois, *Le Catholicisme au féminin: Les congrégations françaises à supérieure générale au XIXe siècle* (Paris: Éditions du Cerf, 1984), is the definitive study of the resurgence of Catholic women's religious orders in France in the nineteenth century.

4. Rebecca Rogers, "Retrograde or Modern? Unveiling the Teaching Nun in Nineteenth-Century France," *Social History* 23, no. 2 (May 1998): 147.

5. Such was the case of the Congrégation de la Mère de Dieu, which solicited Napoleon's help in establishing a school for orphaned cotton mill workers (ibid., 150).

advantage since it provided him with a cadre of teachers willing to recognize the state's authority over education in exchange for the right to resume, or begin, their teaching mission.[6]

Both the reformers of the Revolution and Napoleon undertook initiatives in secondary education for boys. The Revolutionaries created *écoles centrales* (central schools), located throughout the country but administered from Paris, with an ambitious curriculum that included history, literature, languages, science, mathematics, and the arts, designed to form citizens for the new republic. As J. David Markham points out, these central schools had limited success because there were not enough teachers to staff them and pupils did not have the basic skills to take advantage of them.[7] Napoleon is best remembered for creating the *lycée*, an elite male institution for the training of future bureaucrats and military leaders of the empire and the ancestor of the modern French *lycée* (upper secondary school). Like the Revolutionaries, he gave little thought to elementary education or to girls' education beyond the elementary level.[8] Napoleon felt strongly that girls should only be prepared for a life in the home and suggested that convents, as well as public schools, only provide instruction in "religion and assorted domestic skills necessary for the attraction of husbands."[9] Because it was believed that boys and girls required fundamentally different training, separate schools for girls and boys were the ideal. At the beginning of the century, however, there were simply not enough teachers or schools to provide for the entire school-age population.

The governments that followed the Empire in the first half of the century made important improvements in elementary education. The education ministry of the Bourbon Restoration called for the creation of one elementary school per commune to serve all children. Under the July Monarchy of Louis-Philippe, the Loi Guizot of 1833 not only furthered the creation of elementary schools throughout the country but established in the more

6. Doyle, "Catholic Church and State Relations," 111–13.

7. J. David Markham traces the history of Napoleon's educational initiatives in relation to the Catholic Church in "The Revolution, Napoleon, and Education," *The Napoleon Series: Nineteenth-Century Society*, accessed May 25, 2021, https://www.napoleon-series.org/research/society/c_education.html.

8. Markham explains that both Napoleon and the Revolution envisaged the need for normal schools to train teachers for the *écoles centrales* and the *lycées*. Napoleon also created the Imperial University, which was not a teaching institution but, rather, "the body charged exclusively with instruction and public education throughout the Empire." In other words, this was a central ministry of education.

9. Ibid., under "Napoleon."

populous regions the *école primaire supérieure* (upper elementary school), which provided three years of study beyond the primary level.[10] The law also established a system of teacher certification that allowed local councils to award a *brevet de capacité* (teaching certificate) to anyone over eighteen with the proper knowledge and good moral character or to accept prior teaching experience as evidence of teaching ability.[11] The Loi Guizot resulted in the entry of large numbers of Catholic religious into both public and private schools as well as the creation of new Catholic schools.[12] According to Doyle, after 1830, "the Church had a monopoly in the primary sector and had got a foothold in public secondary education through the schools of the teaching orders of brothers."[13]

A further expansion of Catholic education, one especially important for girls, was made possible by the Falloux Law of 1850.[14] Written by representatives from all of France's major religions as well as government ministers, the Loi Falloux solved the problem of separate public schools for girls. Named after the Second Republic's minister of education, Count Frédéric-Alfred-Pierre de Falloux, the Falloux Law called for the creation of a separate elementary school for girls in each commune. Like the Loi Guizot, it recognized that the preparation nuns received in the novitiate was equivalent to that offered by the state normal schools and authorized nuns to teach if they obtained a *lettre d'obédience* (letter of obedience) from their superiors granting them permission to teach. Doyle notes that after 1850 religious schools for girls made substantial gains in enrollment, even as compared to private lay schools.[15] Grew and Harrigan attribute this popularity of Catholic education to the

10. Ministère de l'Éducation nationale, de la jeunesse et des sports, Loi sur l'instruction primaire, Loi Guizot du 28 juin 1833, https://www.education.gouv.fr/loi-sur-l-instruction-primaire-loi-guizot-du-28-juin-1833-1721.

11. Title 2, article 4, of the Loi Guizot specifies that teachers could be certified by passing an examination administered by the local council. It also accepted preparation from normal schools for male teachers. Priests also had a system of normal schools called "petits séminaires" (little seminaries). Nuns normally received the appropriate training during their novitiates to qualify them to teach.

12. I am grateful to Grew and Harrigan, "Catholic Contribution," for explaining the nineteenth-century meaning of public and private schools. *Public* referred to schools supported by the commune, department, or national government, while *private* indicated funding from other sources. Both religious and laics could teach in public schools in the mid-nineteenth century.

13. Doyle, "Catholic Church and State Relations," 113.

14. For details of the Loi Falloux, see "Loi Falloux," Psychologie, éducation & enseignement spécialisé, accessed May 28, 2021, dcalin.fr/textoff/loi_falloux.html.

15. Doyle, "Catholic Church and State Relations," 115.

new requirements for teaching certification. Candidates were now obliged not only to undergo academic training but also to have three years of previous teaching experience before being recognized as *instituteurs* (elementary school teachers): Nuns and priests automatically met these qualifications.[16] The popularity of Catholic schools lasted until the passage of the Jules Ferry Laws in the 1880s, which made elementary education free, obligatory for all children between the ages of six and thirteen, and secular, thereby removing religious education from the daily curriculum and placing religious schools under the control of local authorities.[17] The 1881 Loi Camille Sée finally established free public secondary education for girls. While the Jules Ferry Laws did not destroy Catholic education, which still attracts French students in the twenty-first century, they effectively transformed Catholic schools into private, fee-charging institutions that had to compete with the free public system.[18] Doyle calls 1850 to 1870, the two decades from the passage of the Loi Falloux to the uprising of the Commune, the "zenith of Catholic education" in France.[19] It was during the period of the Loi Falloux that the French Ursulines undertook the first major revisions to their two-century-old teaching method.

THE REVISED *RÈGLEMENTS*

According to St. Jean Martin, the Ursulines survived the French Revolution but in much diminished numbers.[20] The two original Paris convents had been destroyed. Of the three hundred convent schools that existed prior to 1789, only one hundred remained twelve years later, in 1801.[21] Our best source for information on when the Ursulines returned to teaching and where they did so comes from the letters of approbation and the foreword that open the 1860 *Règlements*. The foreword tells us that the Ursulines had begun teaching

16. Grew and Harrigan, "Catholic Contribution," 218.

17. For a résumé of these laws, see "Dossier d'histoire: Les lois scolaires de Jules Ferry," Archives du Sénat, accessed May 12, 2021, www.senat.fr/evenement/archives/D42/1882.html.

18. French Catholic girls attended convent schools well into the twentieth century. One of the best-known graduates of such schools was the philosopher, novelist, and author of *The Second Sex*, Simone de Beauvoir, who reflects upon her education *chez les bonnes soeurs* (with the nuns) in the first volume of her autobiography, *Mémoires d'une jeune fille rangée* (Memoirs of a Dutiful Daughter), of 1958.

19. Doyle, "Catholic Church and State Relations," 118.

20. Ibid., 110. Doyle states that the Ursulines, along with the Christian Brothers, emigrated during the Revolution and did not return until 1803.

21. St. Jean Martin, *Ursuline Method*, 295–97.

THREE CENTURIES OF GIRLS' EDUCATION

over fifty years earlier, that is, shortly after the reconciliation of France and the Vatican allowed them to do so.[22] The letters of approbation signed by bishops from Arras in the north to Toulon in the south, from Dijon in the east to Nîmes in Provence, but not from the city of Paris, indicate that the Ursulines had moved from the capital to the provinces. Both the bishops' letters and the foreword refer to recent editions of the *Constitutions* of 1640 and the 1705 *Règlemens*, in which only the spelling and punctuation had been modernized.[23] Their fidelity to their founding documents demonstrates that the Ursulines considered cloister essential to their mission and would maintain their schools within the convent walls. They sought only to change those points of the teaching program that were no longer useful or no longer conformed to "les exigences du siècle" (the requirements of the times [5]).

The revised edition of the *Règlements des religieuses Ursulines de la Congrégation de Paris, divisés en trois partis, première partie* was published in Clermont-Ferrand in 1860 by Ferdinand Thibaud.[24] The foreword cites the authorization granted by Pope Paul V in 1612 as justification for modifying the original regulations. We do not know the names of the nuns who undertook the revisions, as they identify themselves merely as *on* (we) in the document's foreword. We do know that, from start to finish, the project involved all Ursuline mother superiors. The revisers began by surveying the superiors of every convent to assess the relevance of the 1705 *Règlemens*. Once they had drafted revisions, they presented them to the same superiors, who had the opportunity to review the work and comment on the changes. They only submitted the revised document to their bishops, whose approval they required, after receiving the consent of the superiors. Of primary importance was their resolve to save "tout l'esprit si plein de sagesse, si éminemment religieux des anciens *Règlements*, et de ne rien enlever d'essentiel au fond primitif" (all of the spirit so full of wisdom, so eminently religious of the old Regulations, and to take away nothing essential from the original content [3–4]). The letters of approbation signed by the bishops enthusiastically endorsed the

22. *Règlements des religieuses Ursulines de la Congrégation de Paris* (Clermont-Ferrand: Ferdinand Thibaud, Libraire, 1860), 3. I cite all further references by page number in the text.

23. St. Jean Martin gives the date and place of the final reprinting of the 1705 regulations as 1845 in Clermont-Ferrand (*Ursuline Method*, ix n. 13). There is no date given for the new edition of the *Constitutions*, although the first letter by the bishop of Clermont states that it was done shortly before the revision of the *Règlements* was undertaken. It is reasonable to assume that the publishing house was in Clermont-Ferrand, where the revised *Règlements* was published.

24. This edition of the *Règlements* was reprinted in Clermont-Ferrand a second time in 1895.

modifications as necessary to the success of the Ursuline teaching mission and as consistent with the 1640 constitution. The bishop of Clermont went so far as to quote the 1640 constitution in his praise of the revisers' success in emulating the spirit of the founding documents:

> Sous son nouveau vêtement, l'esprit de l'institution reste et paraît aussi pur, aussi saint, aussi dévoué qu'il l'a toujours été; et on peut dire de ces dispositions qui ont une apparence de nouveauté, ce qui est dit dans la dernière édition des Constitutions: *que les nouvelles sont les anciennes et les anciennes sont les nouvelles.* (i)

> Beneath this new attire, the spirit of the institution remains and appears as pure, as saintly, and as devoted as it has always been; and we could say about these arrangements that give the appearance of novelty what was said in the latest edition of the Constitutions: *what is new is old and what is old is new.*[25]

The 1860 *Règlements* is marked by tension between the determination to reproduce, as closely as possible, the 1705 *Règlemens* and the need to accommodate the "exigences du siècle." Fidelity to the original meant preserving not only its content but also the order of chapters and even the original vocabulary or turns of phrase, unless they were no longer comprehensible to nineteenth-century readers (4). We find a striking—and confusing—example of direct repetition of the 1705 text in the title of the revised document: *Règlements des religieuses Ursulines de la Congrégation de Paris, divisés en trois livres.* The 1705 text did indeed have three parts, two dealing with the schools and a third on cloister. But there is no mention of monastic life in the 1860 text. It has only two parts, the first on the boarding school and the second on the day school. The revisers seem to have kept the original title to suggest how strictly they had adhered to the 1705 *Règlemens* and then clarified their intention to study only the pedagogical system by adding "première partie" (first part).

The title is not the only example of word-for-word repetition of the language found in the 1705 *Règlemens*. The chapters dealing with the duties and schedules of the general mistress, bursar, linen mistress, converse nuns, and pupils read much the same as the original text. Moreover, the chapters

---

25. *Constitutions des religieuses de Sainte Ursule de la Congrégation de Paris* (Paris: Chez Gilles Blaizot, près de la Porte S. Marcel, 1640), 8.

follow the same order in the 1860 edition as in the 1705 one, beginning with the general organization of each school and ending with the regulations governing pupils. The nineteenth-century Ursulines would have found all of this familiar.

When the revisers did change the original language, they often did so through deletions from or additions to the 1705 chapters. These are easy to miss because the revisers do not draw our attention to them. The chapter on the *boursière*, for example, no longer mentions the need for an intermediary to convey the bursar's list of supplies to merchants. The rules of cloister had relaxed enough to allow direct communication between the bursar and her suppliers.[26] The 1860 chapter on the "Règlements des pensionnaires," like the 1705 version, only allows boarders to sleep away from the convent in exceptional circumstances, such as a death in the family. The final paragraph of this chapter, however, authorizes one day a month of "sortie générale" (day off for the whole school) as well as between six weeks and two months of vacation a year so that boarders could have more frequent contact with their families (123). Such slight additions or eliminations did nothing to violate the spirit of the original regulations and brought them in line with the actual practices of nineteenth-century Ursuline boarding schools.

In addition to these changes, it was necessary to update spelling, capitalization, and punctuation, all of which had changed considerably since the seventeenth century. The revisers also tried to make the text more readable by bringing together "divers articles se rapportant au même sujet . . . qui étaient disséminés (various points dealing with the same subject that were spread [throughout the book] [4]). Thus, both chapter two, "Règles générales pour toutes les maîtresses employées au pensionnat" (General Rules for All Teachers Employed in the Boarding School [19–22]), and chapter seven, "Règlement des maîtresses de classe" (Regulation of the Class Mistresses [68–78]), begin with the general injunctions to avoid conflicts and use instruction time wisely that were formerly repeated in separate chapters on the duties of each mistress. The daily schedule prescribed in the original regulations, which always placed reading as the first class of the day, became optional, so that different schools could determine how to organize their day. As long as teachers spent the appropriate time on each subject, the foreword explains, they did

26. Leo XIII, in the New Code of Canon Law of 1918, made this rule of modified cloister official (Monica, *Angela Merici*, 359). The 1860 *Règlements* suggests that this lessening of strictures had already occurred de facto by 1850.

not violate the spirit of the Ursuline mission. This flexibility, in fact, could help schools in different locations conform more appropriately to the customs and needs of their communities (4).

The regulations that required substantive revision and new approval involved the organization of the teaching faculty in the boarding school. The surveys conducted among the mother superiors had indicated that one of the least observed rules was the requirement of a team of two class mistresses for every class who would rotate duties weekly. Large enrollments, as well as the need to learn and prepare lessons in new academic areas, had made it impossible for class mistresses to see to the physical and spiritual needs of their charges and teach while fulfilling their obligations to the religious life. This problem led to the most significant change in the *Règlements:* the creation of large divisions of pupils grouped according to age and ability. Divisions, in turn, would be subdivided into as many classes as necessary to preserve the number of eighteen to twenty pupils per class (11–12).

A new category of teaching nuns, called "maîtresses de division" (division mistresses), was created to take charge of these large groups of pupils. The division mistresses took on the nonacademic duties of overseeing sleeping quarters and meal times, cleaning and dressing younger boarders, and training the older boarders in hygiene, homemaking, and etiquette that in the 1705 regulations had been the responsibility of the class mistresses who were "en semaine." The division mistresses were also charged with all aspects of religious education, including classes devoted to catechism, liturgy, and preparation for the sacraments. The foreword explains that the new category of teaching nuns was made necessary by the evolution in meaning of the word *class,* which, by the late nineteenth century, had come to denote not a group of pupils but, rather, "les leçons d'un professeur particulier" (the subjects taught by an individual teacher [6–7]).

A second group of nuns, called "maîtresses d'instruction, d'enseignement ou, plus simplement de classe" (mistresses of instruction, lessons, or simply, class mistresses), taught all other subjects. There were two categories of class mistresses, those who had their own classroom and those who moved among the classrooms to teach a single subject such as penmanship (13–14). An additional reason for this division of responsibilities was that it was the only way to prevent school duties from overwhelming the commitment to the religious life. It allowed the Ursulines to be "des religieuses, qui doivent rester telles avant tout, et remplir en outre, leurs devoirs et exercices conventuels" (nuns, who must, above all, remain nuns and fulfill, moreover, the duties and practices of convent life [5]). Since the day schools had no need of divisions or division mistresses to care for girls outside of class, they continued the practice of dividing girls according to age and ability into classes in which one class mistress or a team of two mistresses covered all religious instruction and the basic skills of reading, writing, arithmetic, and handwork (152). As in the past, *dixainières* acted as teaching assistants in the day schools.

The revisers understood that numbers of boarders and available teaching faculty would vary from convent to convent. They added flexibility to the new divisional structure by giving schools the choice to assign either a single mistress or a two-mistress team to the new divisions. While the foreword states that the team of two mistresses is preferable in big boarding schools with large student populations and awkward in smaller ones, schools could choose either system. Each had its advantages and problems. Two mistresses could provide more specialized instruction but might disagree with each other and subject pupils to contradictory influences. A single mistress would offer more limited subject matter but might confuse her pupils less. Rather than rely on numbers alone, the general mistress of the boarding school, in consultation with the division mistresses, was encouraged to consider what best fit the school, given its "vues, son experience, et son personnel" (its opinions, its experience, and its personnel [8]). Because the revisers felt it would make the new edition unnecessarily long if they wrote concurrent chapters explaining each system, they only described the method with two mistresses in the chapters of the *Règlements* but provided detailed footnotes to every chapter for mistresses working alone.

One important change not mentioned in the foreword but addressed in several chapters is the financing of both boarding and day schools. In the seventeenth and eighteenth centuries, noble patronage allowed Ursulines to run free schools. Although the families of girls in the *pensionnat* had always been asked to pay the costs of their daughters' clothing, room, and board, poverty did not make an Ursuline education impossible, either in the boarding or day school. With the fall of the nobility and the confiscation of church property during the Revolution, the nuns lost their main sources of revenue. The 1860 *Règlements* mentions several new sources of income for both the boarding and day schools. The bursar of the boarding school had the right to sell to boarders, at the average retail price of the city where the convent was located, "les fournitures," personal and classroom supplies, whose sale provided money for teachers' needs, library materials, or student prizes (91–92). The first chapter dealing with the boarding school mentions the possibility of accepting "demi-pensionnaires," that is, pupils who ate their midday meal in the boarders' refectory but remained separated from the boarders, to help cover expenses (17). In the day schools, "les enfants plus aisées" (the better-off children) were expected to pay for their education at a rate equal to that charged in the secular schools for boys in their communities (151–52). While the day schools still accepted both rich and poor, they separated paying from nonpaying pupils, with girls who paid receiving "une instruction un peu plus étendue" (a bit more extensive instruction [152]). The general mistress of the day school enjoyed the right to sell notebooks and textbooks to paying pupils and to use the "modique profit qui résultera de la vente de ces objets" (the modest profit that will result from the sale of these objects) to buy supplies for poorer students (160). In the "Observation importante" (Important Observation) concluding the chapters on the day school, the authors recognize this departure from their original rule but also plead for their readers' understanding that they cannot do otherwise:

> D'après l'article 5 du chap. [de la constitution de l'ordre] de la pauvreté, on ne doit rien recevoir pour salaire de l'instruction donnée aux pensionnaires et aux externes. Il est regrettable qu'une triste nécessité ne permet pas d'observer ces . . . points essentiels. Formons des vœux afin que des temps meilleurs ramènent la parfaite pratique des constitutions. (176)

> According to paragraph 5 of the chapter [of the order's constitution] on poverty, we are not to receive any salary for teaching the boarders or the day pupils. It is regrettable that a sad necessity does not allow us to observe these . . . essential points. Let us pray that better times allow us to return to the perfect observance of our constitutions.

Apart from the creation of divisions and a new category of mistresses, the 1860 *Règlements* did little to change life in either the boarding or the day school. The boarding school, where division mistresses continued to pay as much attention to their pupils' physical needs and emotional and social development as to their academic instruction, remained the focus of an Ursuline education. Except for now wearing uniforms (118–19), boarders lived much as they had in eighteenth-century convents. Their daily schedule alternated between lessons and devotions; they acquired habits of good hygiene and etiquette in the dormitories and refectories just as they learned to read and write in the classroom. Boarders and day pupils studied in different parts of the convent and did not intermingle. Meals and recreation for the boarders and a two-hour lunch period for day pupils again broke up the school day. Chapters on the duties of division mistresses and class mistresses repeat the language of the 1705 text directing teachers to treat pupils as a loving mother treats her children; to avoid conflicts, favoritism, and punishment; and to teach virtue through example and constant supervision. As was the case in the seventeenth and eighteenth centuries, pupils were required to address teaching nuns as "Ma Mère" (Mother) to reinforce the "Mother Idea," the foundation of Ursuline pedagogy (117). *Dixainières* still worked as aides for the *externes*. Teachers in the day school were reminded, as they had been in the 1705 regulations, that they were privileged to serve the poor in imitation of Christ.

The subjects receiving the most attention were, as before, religion and reading. The methods used to teach catechism and basic skills also remained largely unchanged. Girls learned by reading aloud and giving proper attention to pronunciation, punctuation, and intonation, just as they had in earlier centuries. Catechism class, as in the past, insisted upon understanding church dogma. The rudiments of arithmetic were still taught using objects, including jetons, to count. Penmanship again demanded good posture, care of writing materials, progression from individual letters to sentences, and an understanding of punctuation and spacing. Spelling was taught through *dictées*. Handwork, as before, required teachers to guide young hands in stitchery if they needed help. Larger classes did not excuse mistresses from using discussion and class participation as their principal means of instruction.

At times, greater numbers worked to the benefit of both teachers and pupils. Because it was often impossible to give each division its own refectory or recreational area in the boarding school, the revised regulations allowed for communal rooms, such as refectories where all boarders took their meals, study halls where mistresses from different divisions took turns supervising pupils, or a single indoor recreation space. The description of this last area as "une vaste salle uniquement destinée aux jeux et aux exercices du corps" (an immense room used only for games and physical exercise [15]) suggests that the recreation area was evolving into a gymnasium and the games played there into sports. In the formation of classes within divisions, mistresses now had the right to group girls not only by age but also "d'après le degré de leurs connaissances" (according to the degree of their knowledge [12]), a further division that made it easier for teachers to address individual needs.

The revisions to the 1705 regulations allowed the Ursulines to preserve the most important features of their two-century-old schools and teaching method—the organization of pupils by age and ability; individual attention; and the Mother Idea—while introducing the flexibility necessary to handle larger groups and bring more subjects into the curriculum. The decision to "laisser facultatifs différents points et de ne pas fixer l'ordre et les heures des exercices de la journée . . . [a laissé] aux diverses communautés la faculté de disposer ces mêmes exercices selon les usages et les besoins des localités" (leave different points optional and not to determine the order and times of daily exercises . . . has given the various communities the ability to arrange these exercises according to the customs and needs of their locality [4]). This flexibility recognized not only the varied needs of the pupils but also the varied personalities and talents of the teachers.

THE 1860 CURRICULUM

The first chapter of part 1 gives us a general idea of the organization of the boarding school. If 120 girls were enrolled in the school, they would be grouped according to age and ability into four divisions of approximately 40 pupils each, except for the youngest pupils, whose division would be less numerous. The chapters on the duties of the division mistress and the class mistresses tell us that the youngest pupils were ten years old or younger and that girls in the upper divisions could be fifteen or older. The divisions were intended to facilitate religious instruction and care of the boarders, and girls moved from lower to higher divisions as they became older. For subjects taught by the class mistresses, girls were placed "d'après le degré de leurs connaissances en cinq, ou six, ou sept classes ou cours, plus ou moins selon leur nombre" (according to the degree of their knowledge, into five or six or seven classes, more or fewer depending on the number of pupils [12]). This was a way of keeping classes to the manageable size of eighteen to twenty pupils as well as a means of keeping girls with similar intellectual maturity together. Appendix B, on "les matières de chaque classe" (the subjects in each class), fleshes out this general plan of five, six, or seven classes with the description of a seven-year program of increasingly more advanced instruction in language arts, history, geography, science, and arithmetic (133–37). All Ursuline schools did not necessarily offer a sixth or seventh year of instruction, but if there were enough older pupils to justify these advanced classes, the *Règlements* outlined a curriculum for them. Grew and Harrigan have found that by midcentury the majority of children throughout France were in elementary school for an average of seven years.[27] The 1860 *Règlements* tells us that the Ursuline arrangement did not deviate from the national pattern.

The foreword to the *Règlements* gives a second reason for making fewer demands on classroom teachers in the boarding school, namely the need to teach basic subjects like reading and arithmetic in greater depth and to add more subjects to the curriculum: "maintenant les exigences du siècle, auxquelles il est nécessaire de se conformer dans une sage et juste mesure, veut qu'elle [l'instruction] soit plus étendue et qu'elle embrasse un plus grand nombre de connaissances" (now the demands of our century, to which we must conform in a wise and reasonable measure, require that we provide more extensive instruction and that education include more areas of knowledge [5]). Both chapter seven, dealing with the duties of the class mistresses, and appendix B give us a good idea of how the nineteenth-century Ursulines addressed these demands.

Learning to read still involved making connections between the written and spoken word and extensive oral reading in the classroom, but it was no longer necessary to begin with Latin before attempting to read French. For the boarding school, the 1860 *Règlements* authorized reading "soit du français, soit du latin ou des manuscrits" (either in French, Latin, or handwritten documents [72]).[28] Most day pupils read in French, with only the most capable attempting Latin or manuscript (171). Reading now involved not only the acquisition of literacy but also the mastery of *orthographe* (spelling), which

27. Grew and Harrigan note that this evolution of the French elementary school was independent of the laws passed and that the average of seven years was valid for all types of French elementary schools, whether public, private, Catholic, lay, separate-sex, or *mixte* ("Catholic Contribution," 211–12).

28. According to Chervel, the main thrust of the nineteenth-century elementary schools was to propagate the use of the French language, which, on the eve of the Revolution, was either not the language of six million people or barely spoken by another six million (*Histoire*, 14). The Ursulines were aware of this national initiative and emphasized French, even though they allowed teachers to begin with Latin if they so desired. The use of handwritten texts, or even texts using seventeenth-century spelling, authorized in the chapter on the class mistresses (72), allowed pupils to read older texts as well as those not in print.

had changed considerably over two centuries, and an understanding of grammar.[29] Both grammar and spelling were taught through daily *dictées*, which were subsequently corrected in class, analyzed for mistakes, and the revised sentences written on a blackboard for pupils to copy. Appendix B shows that over the course of seven years, boarders learned the parts of speech and punctuation but also more sophisticated grammatical concepts such as the concordance of verb tenses and the proper use of participial phrases. In the final year, spelling included a study of the trouble points of the French language, such as synonyms and homonyms. Reading, spelling, and grammatical analysis were now brought together under the category of French.

Arithmetic remained practical, concentrating on the fundamental operations of addition, subtraction, multiplication, and division. However, pupils were gradually introduced to more difficult concepts and calculations. Instead of learning simply to write both Arabic and Roman numerals, in their second year girls were taught *numération parlée et écrite*, that is, to transcribe numbers dictated orally into both systems. Girls in the higher classes were expected to master the metric system of weights and measures created in 1790, during the French Revolution, and learn percentages and fractions. In their final years, they were introduced to business concepts such as interest rates and discounts, all of which would help them as managers of their household budgets. The invention of the blackboard allowed the mistress to perform calculations and explain the steps used to solve problems before the whole class. Girls were also expected to explain how they had arrived at answers (77–78). *Ouvrage manuel* demanded mastery of knitting, mending, and dressmaking—all skills required of a wife and mother—before pupils could learn more artistic needlework, such as embroidery (82–83). As in the seventeenth century, penmanship was taught as calligraphy, but in the two advanced years, girls learned round script and Gothic lettering as well as cursive.

The secondary schools for boys envisioned during the Revolution had already included the study of history, geography, science, and the arts as

29. Chervel explains that it is not possible to pinpoint a date when French spelling changed. The changes happened gradually from the 1600s until the mid-nineteenth century. Nevertheless, in the sixth edition of the *Dictionnaire de l'Académie française* of 1835, we find the first complete record of French vocabulary in its modern spelling (Chervel, *Histoire*, 94). The introduction of grammar into the study of the French language did not happen until the end of the nineteenth-century, and even then, there was no distinct French grammar until 1902, when the *explication de texte* was introduced (63). The grammar taught in the Ursuline schools was limited to an understanding of the parts of speech and to the practical use of difficult verbal constructions to composition.

necessary to the formation of civic leaders. Napoleon recognized the importance of science as well as languages and literature in the *lycée* curriculum. By the 1830s, French elementary schools also offered study beyond the basic skills. The Loi Guizot specified geometry, surveying, an introduction to the physical and natural sciences, singing, and history and geography, especially the history and geography of France, as appropriate subjects in the *classes primaires supérieures*.[30] The Loi Falloux endorsed the same elementary curriculum as the Loi Guizot, adding only "la gymnastique" (physical fitness) to the general schedule and the requirement that girls' schools teach "le travail à l'aiguille" (needlework).[31] Appendix B of the 1860 *Règlements* indicates that the expanded Ursuline curriculum mirrored that recommended by the Loi Falloux and included literature, history, geography, science, and singing. This was a conscious choice, since Catholic schools were not obliged to follow the Falloux program. As Rogers has shown in her study of the Congrégation de la Mère de Dieu, other Catholic girls' schools concentrated on vocational training.[32] The Ursulines preferred a general introduction to the arts and sciences that did not preclude the study of practical subjects, such as budgeting and sewing.

The brief paragraphs devoted to these new subjects in chapter seven demonstrate how the nineteenth-century Ursulines succeeded in justifying these new academic areas without departing from their original mission of forming Christian women. In the 1705 *Règlemens*, there is no mention of literature, such as poetry, theater, or fiction. The 1860 regulations acknowledge that while literature is not essential to a girl's education, it is useful in developing "le goût du beau, aussi bien que l'amour du vrai et du bon" (a taste for the beautiful as well as love for what is true and good [73–74]). To encourage an appreciation of literature, teachers read fables and simple poetry to very young girls even before the girls themselves could read. Once girls had learned to read, they concentrated on epistolary works, such as the letters of Mme de Sévigné. History texts were considered admissible literature, but imaginative literature, like novels, was forbidden, as was any contemporary literature whose vocabulary and unusual narrative techniques the *Règlements* derided as "le néologisme moderne" (the affectation of novelty [74]). Seventeenth-century literature offered the model of good literature in

30. Loi Guizot, title 1, article 1.
31. Loi Falloux, title 2, chapters 1 and 5.
32. Rogers, "Retrograde or Modern," 164.

its simplicity and clarity.[33] We see the influence of French neoclassicism in the essay topics assigned in literature class. Mistresses were warned to "ne . . . traiter que rarement des sujets purement d'imagination" (only rarely deal with purely imaginative subjects) but, rather, to prefer topics "qui naissent des faits, des incidents actuels, accoutumant ainsi les élèves à observer et à décrire avec naturel ce qui est sous les yeux" (that are born of facts, of contemporary incidents, thus accustoming pupils to observe and describe with naturalness what is before their eyes [75]). Chervel notes that this type of composition, developed by the Ursulines and Christian Brothers, was adopted throughout French elementary schools because of its value in teaching practical writing, such as contracts.[34] In the Ursuline schools, these compositions were critiqued and corrected by the teacher before the whole class and, if worthy enough, served as *dictées* for younger classes.

From the time of the Revolution, educators considered the study of history a means of instilling patriotism and thus vital to civic education.[35] The *Règlements* justifies history for its intellectual and spiritual potential: it helped form "le coeur et le jugement" (heart and judgment [75]), but the Ursulines were also aware that history could be used to reinforce a Catholic interpretation of civilization. French history concentrated on "les beaux règnes" (the inspiring eras), such as the medieval era, and spent little time on modern French history. During seven years of study, girls devoted as much time to ancient, Roman, and church history as to that of France.

Geography helped girls understand their place in the world. To this end, geography class required knowledge of longitude and latitude, maps, and continents as well as the physical geology, economy, and political divisions (for example, communes, departments) of France. To help the youngest girls grasp abstract concepts such as longitude and latitude, the *Règlements* recommended a method called "la géographie en action" (geography in action), which asked girls to stand around the classroom in imitation of the distances between cities on the map. Older girls filled in maps with lines of longitude and latitude, placing cities along these lines (76). In the upper classes, geography branched into astronomy, for which girls received an in-

33. For Chervel, the importance accorded to the French literature of the seventeenth century in the first half of the nineteenth century reflected an obsession with Latin literature in French education (*Histoire*, 61).

34. Ibid., 60.

35. Markham, "French Revolution."

troduction to geometry as a means of understanding the distances between stars and planets.

Science, like history, stayed clear of controversial topics, especially zoology, undoubtedly to avoid discussion of sex and, perhaps, evolution. The *Règlements* counsels teachers to bring "une grande réserve" (great reticence [77]) to such subjects. Obvious principles of physics, such as gravity, as well as those of botany and minerology, which demanded little more than memorization, constituted the study of science. In this approach, the Ursuline curriculum was no different from the "notions des sciences physiques et de l'histoire naturelle applicables aux usages de la vie" (notions of the physical sciences and natural history that are applicable to everyday life) authorized by the Loi Guizot and unchanged in the Loi Falloux.[36]

For the nineteenth-century Ursulines, the addition of singing to the curriculum meant, above all, the possibility of teaching "chant religieux" (sacred song). This was a significant departure from the custom observed in cloistered communities of allowing only nuns to sing during religious ceremonies. It provided a way of counteracting the appeal of secular art in young imaginations:

Le chant religieux étant très propre à détourner les jeunes personnes de la musique profane et des chansons frivoles, ainsi que l'exprime le pape Paul V dans la bulle d'érection de la maison de Bordeaux, il est très convenable qu'il soit cultivé et en honneur dans les pensionnats d'Ursulines. (84)

Sacred song has the ability to divert young people's attention from profane music and frivolous songs, as Pope Paul V said in this bull establishing the Bordeaux convent. Thus, it is very appropriate to cultivate sacred song and to accord it a place of honor in Ursuline boarding schools.

The revised *Règlements* assigned a special mistress to teach boarders to read music and train them in choral singing. If possible, another nun accompanied the chorus on a musical instrument. The ability to sing the liturgy and hymns was considered so beneficial that girls in the day school received musical instruction "par forme de récompense lorsqu'elles se seront bien appliquées à leurs devoirs" (as a reward when they have applied themselves to their schoolwork [174 n. 1]).

36. Loi Guizot, title I, article 1.

Boarders could also have private lessons in drawing, painting, musical instruments, and foreign languages if their parents wished to pay for them. Chapters on the duties of the teaching mistresses and appendix C, "Règlement de la journée ou ordre des exercices" (Regulation on the Schedule of Classes in the School Day or the Order in Which Classes May Be Taught [146–49]), provided direction on managing such a packed curriculum. Arithmetic and penmanship could be taught on alternate days; related subjects such as history and geography, history and literature, or grammar and spelling could be taught as a single unit; instruction in needlework, now called "ouvrage manuel" (handwork), could take place after the midday meal as a prolongation of recess, and singing could be combined with evening prayers. Since "les arts d'agrément" (fine arts) and instruction in foreign language usually took the form of private lessons given by secular masters under a nun's supervision, they could only occur during recesses, a time of day that did not interfere with regular classes. It was even possible to skip some subjects. The nota bene at the beginning of appendix B only recommends that science be taught to advanced boarders in large, well-staffed convents. Part 2 of the 1860 *Règlements* indicates that day pupils concentrated on the same subjects as their seventeenth- and eighteenth-century predecessors—preparation for the sacraments, reading, penmanship, arithmetic, spelling, and needlework. Mistresses were always free to introduce other subjects or to give advanced instruction in the basic subjects if a class or even an individual day student could do such work.

RELIGIOUS EDUCATION

It is not possible to talk about religious education simply as an academic subject among others in the Ursuline curriculum. The first sentence of the 1860 *Règlements* repeats the 1705 opening statement that the Ursulines were founded for the upbringing and instruction of girls in convent boarding schools. Chapter five of the 1860 text instructs the division mistresses, those responsible for the care of boarders outside the classroom as well as for classroom instruction, never to forget that "le but de cette instruction est de former dans les élèves une foi solide et raisonnée, devenue si rare de nos jours" (the goal of this instruction is the formation of a solid, well-reasoned faith, so rare in our times [54]). A well-reasoned faith required careful intellectual training and a solid faith, the reinforcement of daily prayer, and spiritual direction. There was nothing reactionary about attributing so much importance to religious education. As Grew and Harrigan remind us, religious education was stipulated by the Loi Guizot, and "in all of France, there were few classes that did not begin each day with prayer, teach some history of the Church and the lives of saints. Many lay teachers included the catechism in their curriculum."[37]

What was taught in catechism class and how it was taught corresponded to the age of the pupils. Those in the youngest division were only required to memorize the catechism and learn their prayers. Mistresses explained important theological concepts, such as sin and the Redemption, in simple terms that aroused the young person's love for God and fear of hell. Girls in the second division spent the year preparing for First Communion. Teachers encouraged even the youngest girls to analyze the catechism for themes, vocabulary, and grammar. This had the triple advantage of obliging pupils to pay greater attention to the lesson, to coordinate their ideas rather than simply memorizing separate elements of doctrine, and to "graver plus fortement dans leur esprit les vérités qu'on leur enseigne" (etch more deeply in their minds the truths they are taught [54]). Catechism study was directed to forming "des affections conformes au sujets" (sentiments appropriate to the subject being considered): "en parlant de la création, on les excitera à remercier Dieu de les avoir créées pour une si noble fin. Si on les entretient des quatre fins dernières, on leur inspirera la crainte de Dieu et de ses jugements" (when speaking of the Creation, [the mistresses] will stimulate the pupils to thank God for creating them for such a noble purpose. If they are discussing the Four Last things, they will inspire fear of God and his judgements [53]).

Girls younger than fourteen studied "histoire sainte" (sacred history) in collections of stories drawn from the Old and New Testaments that ranged from simple résumés of biblical texts accompanied by pictures to actual biblical texts with guides for exegesis (33). Girls over fifteen ended their religious education with a three-year cycle dealing with "le dogme compris dans le Symbole des Apôtres; la morale qui a pour règle et pour base les commandements de Dieu; le culte qui renferme la prière, les sacrements, et les cérémonies saintes" (the dogma contained in the Apostles' Creed; the moral philosophy that has God's commandments for rule and basis; the liturgy, which encompasses prayer, the sacraments, and sacred ceremonies [48]). Religious education for boarders in the most advanced classes also included "petites notions de philosophie," which meant an introduction to logic, questions of doubt and certitude, and metaphysics (136–37). A girl who spent six or seven years in the Ursuline boarding school thus received elementary training in both theology and philosophy. In the larger classes, two division mistresses alternated days, with one teaching only catechism and the other only church or biblical history. If classes were smaller and had only one mistress, she taught both areas of religion on alternate days. The class mistresses of the day school concentrated on catechism instruction but could teach church history if they felt their pupils were able to grasp it. Saturday classes for *externes* were devoted to the study of the biblical texts appearing in the gospel of Sunday's mass (162).

By 1860, nuns were no longer solely in charge of sacramental preparation in their schools. An "aumônier" (chaplain) had full authority to decide which girls were ready to receive the sacraments and to instruct from the diocesan catechism.[38] Division mistresses risked becoming little more than assistants, limited to drilling pupils or correcting homework (33). The Ursulines managed to turn these restrictive circumstances to their advantage. While the 1860 *Règlements* acknowledges that "l'instruction religieuse rentre principalement dans la mission de M. l'aumônier" (religious instruction is principally part of the reverend chaplain's mission), it insists that "nos saintes Constitutions ont néanmoins sagement établi que les maîtresses feront le catéchisme deux ou trois fois la semaine" (nevertheless, our holy Constitutions have wisely established [the rule] that teachers will give catechism lessons two or three times a week [47]). A footnote in the same chapter states that three hours weekly was a minimum, since many convents already gave religious instruction every day (49 n. 1). Religion class was one of the longest of the school day, lasting forty-five minutes. A list of the books recommended for lesson preparation, almost entirely teaching manuals for catechism written in the nineteenth century, indicate that the division mistresses used class time principally to clarify the chaplain's words and to help pupils apply the catechism lesson to their own lives.

Outside of the classroom, the division mistress was a spiritual director. She taught the girls their prayers, helped them perform an examination of conscience, and showed them how to approach the altar for communion. She did not preach at them but, rather, showed them how to overcome their selfish

38. The footnotes on 50–52 list a number of catechisms published in different French cities, which indicates that, as in the seventeenth century, catechisms were particular to each diocese.

inclinations by making small sacrifices, a habit that would serve them well in later life. She also functioned like an individual counselor. The *Règlements* instructs her to meet regularly in private with the girls in her division "pour leur donner quelque exercice de vertu analogue à leur besoin, à leur âge, à leur capacité" (to give them an exercise in virtue appropriate to their needs, to their age, to their ability [32]). These private conversations allowed her to know each girl individually and to follow the girl's spiritual progress more closely.

For boarders, the school year was filled with extracurricular activities that reinforced the centrality of Catholicism to an Ursuline education. Such activities involved girls "aux solennités de l'Église et aux fêtes religieuses en usage dans la maison" (in the solemnities of the church and in the religious celebrations customary in the establishment [31–32]). The liturgical calendar became the basis of the school calendar, which observed not only the traditional religious periods of Christmas and Easter but also the feast days of patron and local saints. On such days, which were numerous, girls sang parts of the mass and hymns with the nuns. They participated in processions that included simple devotional acts, such as placing flowers at the base of statues of Christ or the Virgin. Classes in both schools were canceled on days when High Mass was celebrated, and boarders were treated to special meals and recreational activities for the remainder of the afternoon. Ceremonies also took place within each classroom of the boarding and day schools, where every month pupils drew the name of a saint, who became the class patron for four weeks and was honored by a small altar and hymns sung daily by the pupils (113–14, 173–74). Recognizing the appeal of the arts to a child's imagination and youth's love of festivities, such activities sought to turn girls from "les plaisirs profanes" (profane pleasures) by developing a taste for the rituals and pageantry of the Catholic Church (31–32).

Boarders also had the opportunity to become members of student congregations, or sodalities, whose goal was "former les jeunes filles à la piété en stimulant leur zèle et en leur procurant des grâces précieuses" (to train girls in piety by stimulating their zeal and procuring special spiritual favors for them [60]). Like modern organizations such as the Girl Scouts, pious congregations in Ursuline schools required increasing levels of commitment as girls matured. Each congregation had a distinctive mission. Members of the Congrégation de la Sainte Enfance (Congregation of the Infant Jesus) were required only to pray together daily and to find ways to imitate Christ's example of humility and obedience in their daily lives. The Congrégation des Saints Anges (Congregation of the Holy Angels) involved understanding of the theological doctrines about angels and the development of the virtues of purity, obedience, and fervor associated with angels. Membership in the highest-ranking organization, the Congrégation de Marie immaculée (Congregation of Immaculate Mary), required active imitation of the Virgin's modesty in dress, humility in comportment, charity, and obedience in one's daily behavior (124–33).

Each congregation recognized three degrees of membership. A girl first entered as an aspirant, then became an affiliate, and then, finally, attained the status of full member but only if she could prove herself worthy through ever greater acts of piety and improvement in her conduct. In accordance with the Ursuline emphasis on pomp and festivities, religious ceremonies marked the acceptance of girls into a congregation. Every congregation wore distinctive medals and ribbons and had a separate oratory, special prayers, and day set aside for meetings. The congregants of Immaculate Mary had the right to a monthly retreat. Although the convent chaplain and divisional mistresses acted as advisors, a council of student "dignitaires" (dignitaries) conducted the affairs of each congregation. Membership on the council was limited to full congregants elected by majority vote of their peers. Elections took place twice a year to ensure greater participation by all the girls. Councils were composed of a president, one or more assistants to the president, a secretary, treasurer, and a sacristan responsible for maintaining the oratory. With the exception of the sacristan, the congregational councils presented a list of officers not unlike that we would find on student councils in contemporary American schools. Such congregations not only supported the religious mission of the Ursulines but also gave boarders an opportunity for self-governance that was rare for French girls of this era.

The revised regulations show that a new conception of Ursuline education had developed by 1860. It was no longer enough to teach basic skills and prepare girls for the sacraments. Now the goal was excellence, as the first chapter on the boarding school states clearly:

Une communauté se distingue bien plus par la bonne éducation qu'elle donne que par le nombre même de ses élèves, et il vaut mieux en soi élever un nombre moins considérable de jeunes filles que d'en recevoir trop pour ne leur donner qu'une éducation défectueuse ou incomplète. (15)

A religious community distinguishes itself far more by the excellence of the formation it gives than even by the number of its pupils, and it is preferable to form a smaller number of girls than to take in too many and give them a formation that is defective or incomplete.

Achieving excellence implied the right to limit the number of girls taken into the boarding school. Excellence demanded as well that mistresses have a solid knowledge of any subject they taught and one that meant the mistresses spent much of their time outside of the classroom studying and preparing classes:

La première condition pour bien enseigner, c'est de bien savoir: on ne peut communiquer que ce que l'on possède. Les maîtresses s'efforce-ront donc d'avoir une connaissance claire et précise des matières de leur classe: elles auront soin de préparer leurs leçons, afin de les rendre plus profitables aux élèves et mêmes intéressantes. (68)

The first principle of good teaching is knowledge: one can only com-municate what one knows. The mistresses will therefore make an effort to have a clear and precise knowledge of the subject matter of their classes. They will take care to prepare their lessons in order to make them more profitable for their pupils and more interesting.

Pupils, too, were expected to take their classes seriously. In the 1705 *Règlemens*, we find no mention of schoolwork performed outside of class; rec-reations were a time for play, personal reading, or sewing. In the 1860 text, the daily schedules for boarders provide at least one hour a day for homework and study, and the regulations of the class mistresses indicate that they assigned, collected, and graded homework regularly. In the day school, it was still the general mistress who kept track of academic progress by visiting classes, as was the custom in the eighteenth-century Ursuline boarding school. Nine-teenth-century boarders experienced much more formal evaluations. There was an oral and written test on one subject every week and examinations on all subjects except handwork and penmanship at the end of each quarter.

Testing served not only to help teachers determine the effectiveness of their pedagogy but also provided a means of recognizing a boarder's good conduct and effort. The chapter entitled "Des penitences et des moyens d'émulation" (Punishments and Means of Emulation [100–104]) shows that punishments had more to do with misbehavior or laziness than performance on tests. We find only one paragraph devoted to punishments ranging from bad grades to expulsion, depending on the seriousness of the offense, while the rest of the chapter outlines a system of ever greater rewards for the boarder who did well or at least tried her best. Every week, all the mistresses in each division met with the general mistress to decide which girls deserved to figure on the "tableau d'honneur" (honor roll) either for good conduct or academic success. Religion class was graded like any other academic discipline but carried more weight than other subjects. A pupil's name did not figure on the honor roll if she could not demonstrate excellence in the oral or written examination on these "matières sacrées" (sacred subjects) administered monthly by the mother superior of the convent (34). The main qualifications for the honor roll of good conduct were "la piété, la docilité, la politesse ou charité . . . l'application au travail" (piety, docility, politeness or charity . . . effort in schoolwork [101]). Girls who maintained good conduct for a month received a special ribbon, and they were given a crown of artificial flowers if they maintained their places for the entire school year. Girls with good grades also received prizes every quarter and crowns at the end of the year. The chaplain or the mother general of the boarding school read aloud the names of all honorees in ceremonies before the entire religious community in the convent chapel. Quarterly grade reports also took place in public, but only the good reports were read aloud, to avoid humiliating those who performed poorly. Appendix B of the 1860 *Règlements* also describes an optional means of emulation called *dignités de confiance* (titles of confidence [141–45]). These titles, awarded monthly or quarterly, allowed boarders to preside at table during meals, direct games at recess, or lead their classmates in prayer at the beginning and end of the day. Such simple honors no doubt did much to encourage good conduct and good work.

NINETEENTH-CENTURY CRITICISMS
OF CONVENT EDUCATION

As the foreword makes clear, the 1860 *Règlements* does not propose drastic changes but, rather, codifies the best practices that had evolved over the fifty years since the Ursulines had returned to teaching in France while adding new subjects and developing curricula appropriate for a Catholic girls' school. As such, it gives a starkly different view of nineteenth-century convent education than that found in the opening chapters of *Madame Bovary*, which was published in 1857 and set in the same decade when the revised *Règle-*

ments was composed. Although Flaubert does not name the congregation, his description of convent life for boarders, with its emphasis on religious education in and out of the classroom, suggests that he has the Ursulines in his sights. In the novel, Flaubert points to the nuns as the source for the heroine's overwrought sensuality and imagination. He sees religious art and liturgical ceremonies, readings in devotional manuals and lives of the saints, as encouragements to confuse sexual and spiritual desire: in Flaubert's convent, Emma "gently succumbed to the mystical languor induced by the perfumes of the altar, the coolness of the holy-water fonts, the gleaming of the candles. Instead of following the Mass she kept her prayer book open at the holy pictures with . . . the Sacred Heart pierced by sharp arrows, and poor Jesus stumbling and falling under his cross."[39] Here Flaubert harks back to the criticism voiced by Diderot in *La Religieuse* (written, 1780; published, 1796) that equated celibacy with suppression of the passions and, inevitably, perversion as well as that of Laclos in *Les Liaisons dangereuses* (1782), in which the nuns prepared the young Cécile so poorly for the real world that she does not even realize she has been raped by the libertine Valmont. The *Règlements* shows that, far from an emotional or sentimental approach to religious instruction, the Ursuline method of teaching catechism stressed understanding Christian doctrine, examination of conscience, and self-control. Nor was it true, as Flaubert contends in a later paragraph, that boarders like Emma easily escaped the nuns' surveillance in order to spend free time with a penniless noblewoman who, while sewing for the convent, sang love songs, recounted the latest gossip from the outside world, and smuggled in novels for girls to read surreptitiously. The *Règlements* contradicts every element of this vision: boarders were constantly supervised by either mistresses or converse nuns and were never left alone with visitors; given their schedule of classes and devotions, girls had little time for daydreaming or idle chatter; novels were forbidden. Flaubert was right to warn against the temptations of the nineteenth century, such as the greater availability of material goods and books as well as the access to the theater and opera, that spread the romantic notions of love and adultery even in the provinces. The Ursulines, however, were well aware of such "plaisirs profanes." In the 1860 revised rule, they proposed as countermeasures a curriculum that stressed academics and provided opportunities for community engagement and leadership.

39. Gustave Flaubert, *Madame Bovary*, trans. Francis Steegmuller (New York: Random House, 1992), 41–42.

Flaubert echoes the criticisms of secular educators from the Second Republic through the first decade of the Third Republic who condemned religious boarding schools as dangers to society. Champions of lay public schools did not object to the fact that convents only accepted girls or trained girls for a future as wives and mothers. As Linda Clark explains, all nineteenth-century pedagogical treatises on girls' education insisted that woman's place was in the home.[40] The principal objection was that a convent education made girls into instruments of the Catholic Church rather than of the state and encouraged obedience to God rather than to husbands. Social historian Rebecca Rogers cites, for example, a school inspector's report of 1864 that derides convent education as so far removed from the real world that it "paves the way for future antagonisms within the family."[41] This inspector correctly judged that teaching nuns, while nominally under the control of a priest or bishop, operated outside of the male sphere and offered girls a rare example of women not bound by domesticity.

The anti-clericalism expressed in *Madame Bovary* was a harbinger of the Jules Ferry Laws of the 1880s, which marked the end of the golden age of Catholic education in France. These laws placed all education, whether elementary, secondary, or university, under state control. *Externats*, or day schools, became the standard. Only those trained in secular normal schools were certified to teach. While religious education could take place in the school, it could only do so outside of class hours by clerics who had the approval of government ministries. In place of catechism, schoolgirls received "l'enseignement moral," that is, lessons in citizenship and civic obligations.

In other respects, however, the education for girls mandated by the Jules Ferry Laws differed little from that proposed by the *Règlements* of 1860. Girls and boys still attended separate schools. The goal of girls' education was still homemaking. In the secular schools, girls spent much of the day learning sewing, hygiene, and "économie domestique" (home economics)—skills they would have learned in their daily lives as boarders. The academic subjects—reading, literature, geography, French history, introduction to the physical sciences, foreign languages, music—were almost identical in the

40. Linda L. Clark, "The Primary Education of French Girls: Pedagogical Prescriptions and Social Realities, 1880–1940," *History of Education Quarterly* 21, no. 4 (Winter 1981): 411.
41. Rogers, "Retrograde or Modern," 146.

two systems.[42] The fact that public and Catholic curricula were so similar suggests that the conflicts between the French church and state were more political than pedagogical.[43] The Ursuline nuns were aware of and engaged in the discussions for girls' education of their time, and they created a curriculum that not only prepared girls for leadership in the nineteenth century but also offered an education of high quality. Once again, Angela Merici's prescient demand that the Ursuline method be endowed with the power "to yield to the exigencies of the time and suit itself to the needs of each age" had proven efficacious.

42. *Loi du 21 décembre 1880 sur l'enseignement secondaire des jeunes filles*, Ministry of National Education, France, accessed May 28, 2021, www.education.gouv.fr/cid101180/loi-sur-l-enseigne-ment-secondaire-des-jeunes-filles-21-decembre-1880.html&xtmc=histoiredesarts&xtnp=4&xtcr=58.

43. See William R. Keylor, "Review: Anti-Clericalism and Educational Reform in the French Third Republic: A Retrospective Evaluation," *History of Education Quarterly* 21, no. 1 (Spring 1981): 95–103.

THREE

THE
Ursuline Method
IN THE
Twentieth Century

IN THE COURSE OF THE EIGHTEENTH AND NINETEENTH CENTURIES, Ursuline missionaries had carried Angela Merici's Mother Idea to all parts of the globe. Sister Monica, writing in the 1920s, estimated that by 1900 Ursuline convent schools could be found not only in every European country, America, and Canada but also in Australia, China, Africa, and South America. While there still existed Companies of Saint Ursula—groups of celibate laywomen who lived together and taught without taking formal vows—the majority of Ursulines were congregations of cloistered religious. Over six hundred such convent schools were engaged in the teaching of hundreds of thousands of girls.[1] In an effort to bring together the widespread and independent Ursuline convent schools, Pope Leo XIII asked Ursuline superiors to convene a congress in Rome in 1900. It resulted in the establishment of the Roman Union of the Order of Saint Ursula, which joined over one hundred Ursuline congregations, mostly from Europe and North America, into an international religious order with headquarters in Rome.[2] During the Second

1. Sister Monica, *Angela Merici*, 360.
2. See "Ursulines," *The Catholic Encyclopedia*, vol. U, accessed May 27, 2019, www.newadvent. org/cathen/15228b.htm, for a summary of the foundation of the Roman Order. Sister Monica attributes the formation of the Roman Union to "the nineteenth century with its growing passion for consoli-

World War, the third prioress general of the Roman Union, Mother Marie de St. Jean Martin (1876–1965), emerged as a defender of the traditional Ursuline pedagogy. Her *Ursuline Method of Education* of 1946 argues for the relevance of the Mother Idea in the twentieth century and advocates a return to the traditional teaching method outlined in the 1860 *Règlements* of the Congregation of Paris.

Marie de St. Jean Martin was the most important spokeswoman for Ursuline education in the twentieth century. Born in the Pas-de-Calais region of France in 1876, she joined the order that had educated her in spite of her attraction to the contemplative life. In addition to being a prolific writer on all matters concerning her order,[3] she was involved in pedagogical reforms and administration, first as headmistress of her local school, then as novice mistress and provincial in western France, later as assistant general to the order in Rome, and finally prioress general of the Roman Union, to which position she was elected in 1926.

Among her most significant achievements was the frequent convening of congresses that allowed Ursuline prioresses throughout the world to leave their cloisters and travel to Rome. Like conventions of professional associations today, these congresses provided opportunities for faculty development as well as for the discussion of practical matters, such as changes to the union's constitution. Lectures by prelates kept the nuns informed of contemporary Catholic teaching on subjects as controversial, for example, as the church's opposition to socialism. Congresses often culminated in retreats that reinforced the unified spiritual mission of the order before the superiors returned to their far-flung provinces. St. Jean Martin did not limit her efforts to Ursulines of the Roman Union. In 1935 and 1938, she invited independent Ursulines from Poland and Germany to congresses, and in 1939, she supported a plan to open Ursuline congresses to all religious teaching women from France. "By this frequent contact of the Union with itself and with other Orders and

---

dation and centralization" (351). St. Jean Martin mentions the use of the *Règlements* by the Roman Union in the United States in the 1940s (*Ursuline Method*, 301–3). In the twenty-first century, the Roman Union remains the dominant order of Ursulines.

3. The menology in honor of Marie de St. Jean Martin lists as her most important writings the revision of the Ursuline constitutions and manuals for novices, *The Book of Customs, Directory of Spiritual Exercises, The Spirit of St. Angela, The Ursuline Method of Education,* and frequent letters to her Ursuline daughters. "Mother Marie de St. Jean Martin," Menology for the 28th June (Sacred Heart Convent, Festus, MO, n.d.).

Congregations," St. Jean Martin's eulogizer writes, "the international sense was awakened and fortified in the Union and the idea of competition, which too often existed in former days with regard to other religious families, disappeared of itself."[4] She not only convened Ursulines to Rome but also traveled throughout Europe and the United States in an effort to understand the needs of Ursulines outside of France. In large measure, her erudition, energy, and dedication led to the establishment of a truly international Ursuline order.

St. Jean Martin's travels and her work of organizing conferences provided the occasion for the composition of *The Ursuline Method of Education*. In 1939, in preparation for the celebration of the four hundredth anniversary of the founding of the Ursulines, she undertook an extensive trip to visit the seventy houses of the Ursuline Union in the United States.[5] The culmination of this trip was the Educational Convention of August 18–28, 1940, held at the Ursuline College of New Rochelle—the first Catholic college for women in New York State—where, in addition to lectures by St. Jean Martin herself, speakers from the University of Notre Dame and the French theologian Jacques Maritain spoke. At the conclusion of this general meeting of the Roman Union, unable to return to war-torn Europe, St. Jean Martin went to Missouri, where she spent the remainder of the war years in the Ursuline Central Province. While there, as she explains in the opening paragraphs of her English-language work, she decided to expand and reissue the report of the Educational Convention of 1940, which was no longer in print.[6] Her *Ursuline Method of Education*,[7] however, is much more than a handbook designed for religious instruction. It is, at once, a history and a defense of the oldest and most successful method of Catholic education for girls and young women.

While the war gave St. Jean Martin the time to write her book, the inspiration for *The Ursuline Method of Education* came from her lifelong meditation on the place of Catholic education for women in contemporary society. Her native country of France, under the Jules Ferry Laws of the 1880s, offered the most obvious example of the secularization of education, but conflicts between

4. *In Memoriam. Mother Marie de St. Jean Martin. 3rd Prioress General of the Roman Order of Ursulines, 1926–1959* (Rome: Società Grafica Romana, n.d.), 15–19.

5. Ibid., 32.

6. St. Jean Martin, *Ursuline Method*, v. All further citations from *The Ursuline Method* will be cited in the text.

7. After the war and her return to Rome, Mother St. Jean Martin revised *The Ursuline Method of Education* and rewrote the book in French for a European audience. Five editions *of L'Education des Ursulines* were published in Rome by the Vatican Press between 1944 and 1947.

church and state over control of schools had arisen in other traditionally Catholic countries of Europe, such as Belgium, in the late nineteenth century.[8] The rise of socialist governments in the nineteenth century that were often openly antagonistic to Christianity, the triumph of atheistic communism in Russia and fascism in Germany by the mid-twentieth century, and the culmination of hostilities between European governments and ideologies in genocidal war in the 1940s convinced St. Jean Martin that civilization had descended into social chaos not unlike that of the time of the Wars of Religion, when Angela Merici had established the Ursulines. For St. Jean Martin, a revival of the traditional Ursuline method was a step in the direction of restoring order to society.

She was not the first Catholic voice in this matter. Pope Leo XIII, the author of *Rerum novarum* (1891), the first encyclical to condemn socialism, and *Immortale Dei* (1885), which rejected the authority of the state over the church, also addressed the church-state conflict over public education. In his brief encyclical *Spectata Fides* (On Christian Education) of 1885, the pope recognized the civilizing influence of Catholic teaching on youth from the Middle Ages to the present, extolled Catholic schools for instructing children in faith and morals as well as in academic subjects, and concluded that "there is no better citizen than the man who has believed and practiced the Christian faith from his childhood."[9] Pius XI spoke even more forcefully in favor of the rights of the church in his 1929 encyclical *Divini Illius Magistri* (On the Christian Education of Youth), in which he not only echoed Leo XIII's assertion that there is no conflict between a person of faith and a good citizen but even claimed that Christian education better preserved the authority of the family—which is the foundation of society—than did secular schools. Pius XI rejected coeducation because the needs of boys and girls are so different, and he opposed sex education given by any adult except a parent. He judged instruction in ethics not grounded in Christian teachings as invalid. In the concluding points of the encyclical, Pius XI writes, "For whatever Catholics do in promoting and defending the Catholic school for their children, is a genuinely religious work and therefore an important task of 'Catholic Action,'"[10] a form of social service and means of evangelizing the secular

8. For a résumé of these conflicts, see "Belgium," *Catholic Encyclopedia*, vol. B, accessed January 15, 2020, newadvent.org/cathen/02395a.htm.

9. Article 4, *Spectata Fides*, accessed January 17, 2021, www.vatican.va/content/leo-xiii/en/encyclicals/documents/hf_lxiii_enc_27111885_spectata-fides.html.

10. Article 84, Divini Illius Magistri, accessed January 17, 2021, https://www.papalencyclicals.net/pius11/p11rappr.htm.

world. St. Jean Martin cites both popes frequently in the chapters of her book. She demonstrates the debt she owes to their encyclicals on education most notably in appendix B, entitled "Summary of the Conferences on the Social Order by Rev. G. Desbuquois, S.J." Here she credits the popes from Pius IX through Pius XI for preparing the ground for a new blossoming of Catholic schools: "Leo XIII imposed an integral social doctrine on the entire educational system, from the universities to the smallest catechetical study clubs. ... Pius XI worked for the expansion and for the incorporation of the Mystical Body in all things temporal. ... Actually, it is from the Church, especially from Leo XIII and Pius XI, that the reformers of our unstable social order are now seeking light and help" (324).

While Popes Leo XIII and Pius XI addressed the dangers to the family and society posed by secular schools, the mid-twentieth-century French theologian Jacques Maritain worried about their deleterious effects on the individual child. In a series of lectures delivered at Yale University during World War II, published as *Education at the Crossroads*, he condemned the contemporary tendency in American education to overemphasize the child's relationship to society. He judged educational philosophies, such as pragmatism, that kept religion out of the classroom as failures to recognize man as the only creature endowed with reason. Pragmatism misunderstood the goal of education, which was to develop judgment and strengthen the will, to form independent adults capable of moral action. Maritain concludes that "the ultimate end of education concerns the human person in his personal life and spiritual progress, not in his relationship to the social environment."[11] St. Jean Martin found much in Maritain's thought that she agreed with and that agreed with traditional Ursuline pedagogy, such as his belief in the individuality and dignity of every human being, a belief that required the teacher to know each pupil personally, or the relationship between age and intellectual development, and the superiority of the liberal arts over specialized and vocational training.[12] We find Maritain's influence especially in the emphasis St. Jean Martin places on the study of literature, history, and philosophy in the Ursuline curriculum.

St. Jean Martin did not, however, rely only on papal letters and theology in making her argument for the Ursuline method. She knew the history of her order from the writings of Angela Merici and the seventeenth-century found-

11. Jacques Maritain, *Education at the Crossroads* (New Haven: Yale University Press, 1943), 14–15.
12. Ibid., 9–10, 60–74.

resses of the Congregation of Paris to the nineteenth-and twentieth-century historians of the order. She addresses her readers with a solid understanding of the French Catholic defense of women's education, citing the writings of Monsignor Félix Dupanloup, member of the French Academy and author of treatises on girls' education,[13] who formulated the Falloux Laws of the 1850s; and Madeleine Daniélou, the twentieth-century foundress of the first secondary school in France in which girls could prepare a baccalaureate in classics.[14] She also cites recent experiments in American education, such as the revival of teaching seminars at St. John's College in Annapolis, Maryland, which, like the *Règlements*, downplay competition for grades in favor of general appreciations of a student's work. She was familiar with the teaching practices of Notre Dame University, which relied on close contact between clerical teachers and young men to incorporate spiritual development into the curriculum and extra-curriculum.[15]

The Ursuline Method of Education opens with a quotation from Pius XI that encapsulates Mother St. Jean Martin's argument for the suitability of the traditional Ursuline method in the twentieth century: "Education consists of a well-made synthesis of Tradition and Progress" (v). No pedagogy can succeed without incorporating the wisdom of past teachers, just as no traditional pedagogy can survive without taking into account the changing needs of every new generation of learners, or as the author puts it more succinctly, "To scorn new ways and to reject the past would be contrary to good sense" (249). Fortunately, the ability to adapt was built into the Ursuline project from the time of its inception in the sixteenth century, when Pope Paul III granted Angela Merici and her daughters the right "to yield to the exigencies of the time and suit itself to the needs of each age" in their teaching vocation.

St. Jean Martin reminds us that Angela Merici was herself a progressive because she brought education for girls into the streets. Yet when the Ursulines established themselves in France and understood the advantages of becoming a formal religious order, they were able to accommodate Angela's Mother Idea to the cloister through the formation of mistresses that acted as mothers as well as teachers and with a curriculum focused on religious education (246–50). Appendix A, which traces the influence of the Jesuit *Ratio*

---

13. See *De l'education* (1872) and *Lettres sur l'education des filles et sur les études qui conviennent aux femmes dans le monde* (1879).

14. See especially *L'Education selon l'esprit* (1939).

15. St. Jean Martin, *Ursuline Method*, 83–85, 202.

Studiorum on the Ursuline *Règlements*, suggests that the seventeenth-century foundresses of the Paris congregation adjusted a Jesuit education designed for the religious and intellectual training of adolescent boys into a program that prepared girls of all ages to receive the sacraments while instructing them in basic literacy and numeracy. The authors of the 1860 *Règlements* faced different problems, most importantly the ability to focus on religious education as well as on the personal contact between teacher and pupil in spite of the demands placed on classroom teachers by large numbers of pupils and an extensive curriculum. This problem was solved in large part by the creation of the division mistresses, who both taught religion and supervised the spiritual upbringing of their charges. Yet this revision did nothing to transform Angela Merici's method. "The Ursuline ideal of education," St. Jean Martin tells us, "was, in the seventeenth century, the same as it is now, to train teachers and conduct schools that neglect no useful branch of human knowledge, while they surround students with all the safeguards and helps of religion" (252).

She offers proof of the adaptability of the Ursuline method in three areas: teacher preparation, modification of the curriculum, and community service. In the chapter on "Progress," St. Jean Martin reminds the reader that Angela Merici's own writings took up the matter of teacher training, specifying that older matrons train younger women not only in the content of Christian doctrine but in the appropriate methods for teaching it. We have noted the detailed instructions for teaching different subjects in both the 1705 and 1860 regulations of the Congregation of Paris as well as the clearly stated requirements in these documents that teachers have a strong grasp of their subject matter. The Roman Union perfected this system of teacher preparation by requiring novices to enter provincial juniorates after the novitiate. In addition to Christian doctrine and theology, these "juniors" studied child psychology, engaged in classroom observation, and wrote lesson plans for two years. St. Jean Martin describes the juniorate as a place "where intellectual defects may be remedied. There, over[ly] analytical minds are led to make synthetic judgments; the superficial are encouraged to penetrate beneath the surface; those wanting in mental initiative are deterred from seizing upon every passing opinion" (258–59). The juniorate served thus as a period of intellectual and professional development. It also instilled a love of learning that resulted in a lifetime of study: the Ursuline would naturally want to spend her free time perfecting her spiritual life in retreats or enrolling in summer sessions in Catholic universities to command better the subject she taught. Since the Roman Order was international, St. Jean Martin recommended that, when peace had been reestablished after the war, American Ursulines study in the great Catholic universities of Europe while their European sisters could come to the United States (259–61). These study exchanges served the dual purpose of increasing both knowledge and communication among the disparate congregations.

In *The Ursuline Method of Education*, a solid, general education remains the primary goal. This does not mean that girls received a limited education. Quite to the contrary, St. Jean Martin asserts that girls have the right to study all fields of human knowledge and that depriving them of such opportunities leads young souls into "frivolity, into apathy; they lead selfish lives, bringing destruction to all ideals, to all serious love and virtue" (32)—an argument not unlike that made by Fénelon in the seventeenth century. The Ursuline education was always practical. In the eighteenth-century French convent schools, girls learned to write and to read handwriting, thus gaining a considerable degree of independence. The nineteenth-century *Règlements* recognized that girls needed to know the rudiments of science, geography, and national history to deal with health and legal matters. St. Jean Martin reminds us that the introduction of new subjects in the curriculum, when such subjects are appropriate to the interests of the students, is an Ursuline tradition. She points to the Canadian convent of Trois Rivières, which had developed courses in journalism as early as 1845 to enable the publication of a student magazine. The Quebec convent had even taught architecture in 1834 (62–63). In line with this tradition, she counsels convent schools in rural areas to offer courses in agriculture, a thorough understanding of which will enable the wives of farmers not only to participate in the management of the land but also to become leaders in their rural communities (187). She recommends, moreover, a year of higher education for more ambitious girls. A year spent studying the liberal arts in a Catholic university would also be of practical value in later life. It would inspire in future mothers "a taste for serious reading and a desire to continue such culture in their homes" and make marriage more fulfilling: "Among the few happy things in this world, one of the highest is a conjugal intimacy, which does not end in a community of interests, nor even in affection, but which culminates in the domain of thought" (188–90).

In the section entitled "Social and Apostolic Formation," St. Jean Martin points out that from its inception "The Order of Saint Ursula, founded by Saint Angela, has borne this Catholic, social character in its work as well as in its recruitment" (98). The early companies in Italy accepted women from all classes of society. They refused no girl, rich or poor, an education. The first French congregations provided free day schools for the poor, while the Ursulines in Quebec and Louisiana—arguably the first social workers in the New World—educated the daughters of slaves and indigenous tribes. They considered such service to the larger community consistent with the Catholic doctrine of the Communion of Saints, which sees all humans as equal parts of the Mystical Body of Christ and all dependent on one another. In her argument for the adaptability of the Ursuline method to contemporary notions of community service, St. Jean Martin invokes Pius XI's idea of "Catholic Action," that is, the participation of the laity in the church's work of charity, education, and evangelization. The program she outlines begins in the earliest years of school, when girls are too young to engage in social work but not too young to acquire a social conscience. Elementary pupils should be introduced to the church's teachings on charity and justice, be exposed to the lives of the saints for inspiration, and develop the desire to treat everyone they meet with respect and kindness. In the intermediate classes, girls deepen their understanding of Catholic doctrine. They also engage in simple acts of charity, such as serving meals to the poor under the guidance of nuns or priests. College-age students, however, are expected to engage fully in service to the poor and persecuted. St. Jean Martin specifies that these girls be required to sacrifice their own material comforts to obtain money for their work and then distribute this money to the poor in person. In addition, they should undertake this social service only after a thorough study of the "economic life, social laws, the condition of the workers, and the various solutions to these social problems that have been proposed or tried" in order to avoid contamination by political propaganda. St. Jean Martin formed her program on three foundations of Ursuline education: recognizing the different capacities of different ages, including religious instruction in subjects other than catechism, and training the intellect to firm the will. Having developed "a loyal, disinterested, fraternal, and Catholic spirit," Ursuline alumnae will continue such charity throughout their lives and offer living examples of Leo XIII's contention that there is no better citizen than one who has believed and practiced the Christian faith since childhood (101).

Defenses of the Ursuline method are regularly interspersed with criticisms of secular education. In the opening chapter of part 1, for example, St. Jean Martin counters the "great fallacy of the American system," founded on "a confused notion of democracy, which extended education to all, through compulsory education legislation, without adapting the methods and the curriculum of the school to the needs of the individual" (51). Since every child is different from all others in personality, intellectual capacity, and talent, this "democratic" system based on abstract law, rather than daily contact, fails more children than it helps. Highly intelligent students require different training than average students, and even among the highly intelligent, some are drawn to thought while others to action. Forcing the children of rural and working-class families into the same mold as those from wealthy and urban backgrounds has done more to destroy the family than to reduce social inequality:

Social classification among children has been suppressed but efforts at social leveling have brought sad results. As a result of this leveling, some children have refused to return to their families, where they find life too lowly and too difficult. There have been young girls who, while they were performing manual work at school in payment for tuition which they could not afford, imitated their richer companions by squandering in amusements the little money they had earned instead of using it to help their parents. Have these children been helped? Have they been prepared for a happy or an unhappy future? (52–53)

St. Jean Martin's criticism becomes increasingly sharp when she considers girls' education specifically. Curricula that stress breadth rather than depth of knowledge produce shallowness rather than self-knowledge and self-control: "What attention is actually being given in houses of education to the intellectual development of young girls? They are made to study extensively, to study manifold subjects. But is not the formative value being depreciated by failure to demand accurate thought? Ten or twelve years spent in the superficial study of a number of things, followed immediately by a worldly life, contribute greatly to the levity and vanity of women" (35). A one-size-fits-all system that offers the same preparation for girls and boys also has drastic consequences for society: "The result of this incomplete, although overburdened, education is witnessed in the destruction of the family" (30).

St. Jean Martin also castigates Catholic schools that do not integrate religion into all parts of the school life. She has harsh words for Catholic boarding schools that do not require daily participation in religious services, accusing them of promoting "spiritual anemia" as opposed to the "supernatural vitality" of Ursuline girls. Parochial schools that treat preparation for the sacraments as little more than an academic subject fail in their mission to form Catholic adults because they have no personal relations with their charges:

> Parochial schools are attended by hundreds of day pupils. Is it not possible to give each of these schools a few spiritual mothers? If so, when will pupils be free to see them? These pupils arrive just in time for the beginning of class and return home as soon as it is over. . . . Should the teachers be apathetic? Or will they find ways of having personal contact with their pupils, so that they may help develop each according to her ability? Some of these children will certainly be called by God to form part of a select group and to exercise great influence. Ursulines will be true educators in the measure in which they have this contact. (86–87)

In the chapter that serves as the conclusion of *The Ursuline Method of Education*, St. Jean Martin sums up her criticisms of twentieth-century education. She begins by taking a hard look at the nineteenth-century myth of progress, one that we find in Victor Hugo's *Les Misérables* (1862), according to which the spiritual regeneration of humanity can only come about through education. She asks her readers if such progress has been achieved in the contemporary world, where war, genocide, chaos, and the destruction of the family leave little room for optimism. Modern education systems have played a role in this "retrogression toward paganism" (246), and women have not fared well. Quoting the Jesuit bishop John Canevin, St. Jean Martin reminds us that the Catholic Church has always boasted learned women, some of whom, like Angela Merici, were self-educated and others, in the Middle Ages and Renaissance, who attended universities: "In proportion to the population, there were probably as many women students in the higher schools of France and other European countries in the days of Saint Angela as there are today" (251). Given the similarities between Merici's time and our own, and the success of her method, a return to traditional Ursuline education was well worth a try.

From the opening pages of *The Ursuline Method*, the author makes no secret of her belief that the primary roles of a Catholic laywoman are those of wife and mother. She says this not because she believes that women are inferior to men but, on the contrary, because she sees them as superior in virtue and thus the source of stability in the family and community. St. Jean Martin interprets the Genesis story of creation, in which Eve is created from the side of Adam rather than from clay, as scriptural proof that woman is more human than man and thus less materialistic, more drawn to ideals and religion, "more soul than man" (5–6). Given their moral potential, girls require teachers who know them intimately, who care for both their physical and intellectual needs, who exemplify the virtues they must acquire and help each pupil realize her unique personality. The Ursuline method, like the Jesuit *Ratio Studiorum*, also has pedagogical advantages since its goal is to train the intellect rather than prepare the child for examinations. It encourages girls to give special attention to the subjects for which they have the least aptitude, instead of avoiding such subjects. She terms such intellectual training "formation," which she contrasts with the contemporary emphasis on "information" designed for testing or to prepare girls for specific degrees rather than for a lifetime of learning (264).

This concept of formation dominates the sections of chapter three, "The Method in Action," which deals with the Ursuline curriculum. The academic subjects listed—catechism, classical languages, language arts, literature, history, geography, philosophy, mathematics, and science—are not unlike those in the 1860 *Règlements*. The only class that does not appear is penmanship, which is subsumed under language arts. Catechism class still occupies the place of honor and concerns, above all, Christian dogma: "The children should be taught why we believe in mysteries and should be helped to understand all that they are capable of grasping" (113). The study of one's native language begins with grammar, "an excellent means of forming judgment and good habits of thought," the mastery of which is expressed through correct speech and a clear writing (136–39). Classical languages and literature are essential not only because Greek and Latin are the mother tongues of European civilization but because they "teach man how to think and how to speak by means of the most inspired monuments of thought and of language." These languages are so critical to the development of our understanding that St. Jean Martin insists upon reading classical literature in the original: "Translations . . . are of only mediocre help to their readers, because they are always imperfect; the very essence of their originality is lost" (120–22).

St. Jean Martin's model of the ideal Ursuline institution is the boarding school, which she undoubtedly knew would become less and less common, especially in the United States. Although she does not explicitly talk about the possibilities of preserving the Ursuline method in day schools, she does outline a number of practices that would allow day schools to provide much the same religious formation as boarding schools. She recommends, above all, that a single teacher remain in charge of each classroom. Like the *maîtresse de division*, this teacher would instruct religion and prepare girls to receive the sacraments but also act as a spiritual mother, getting to know each girl personally, spending time with her outside of the classroom, and encouraging examination of conscience, prayer, and frequent reception of the sacraments. Sodalities—another name for the *congrégations* noted in the 1860 *Règlements*—provided girls other opportunities for "progressive spiritual formation" (89), as did retreats, contact with nuns and priests during summer vacations, and charitable activities undertaken with classmates. St. Jean Martin suggests that an Ursuline education could extend beyond graduation through yearly reunions, at which priests offered conferences on religious subjects and guided alumnae in prayer. In this way, Saint Jean Martin tells us, Ursuline teachers "will still wield an influence over their former pupils" (92).

The one point on which St. Jean Martin remained inflexible was the necessity of cloister: "The life of the Ursulines of the Order must be lived in the shadow of the cloister, must have its center in the chapel, where they are to be found seven times a day, not including private visits to the Blessed Sacrament; and they must constitute a community of nuns numerous enough to chant divine office and practice common observances with all the dignity demanded" (278). Although she wrote these lines more than a decade before the Second Vatican Council convened in 1962, she undoubtedly sensed that changes were coming and feared that any dispensation from monasticism would destroy the intense spiritual life that supported Ursulines as they fulfilled their fourth vow. Coming at the end of a detailed book on the history of the order, its educational philosophy and teaching methods, her plea for the necessity of cloister reminded twentieth-century Ursulines that they were, above all, a community of religious women who expressed their faith by educating girls and who could find support for their mission in the original teaching manual of their order, the *Règlements des religieuses Ursulines de la Congrégation de Paris*.[16]

16. Archivist Mary Lee Berner Harris told me, during a visit to Ursuline Academy in New Orleans in August 2019, that after Vatican II released nuns from the obligation of cloister, the New Orleans Ursulines chose to remain together in their convent. In a subsequent telephone conversation, Sister Thomas More Daly, OSU, archivist of the Ursuline Archives of the Central Province, USA, told me that while individual nuns left the order after Vatican II, the American Ursulines stayed together in communities, observing their vows of poverty, chastity, and obedience as well as teaching.

REGULATIONS

OF THE

URSULINE
NUNS

OF THE
CONGREGATION
OF PARIS

DIVIDED INTO THREE PARTS[1]

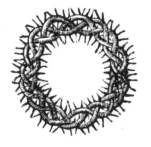

PARIS:
chez LOUIS JOSSE, rue St. Jacques, à la
Couronne d'épines,

1705
with privilege and approval.[2]

1. The "three parts" noted in the title require some explanation. The first book, "The Education of Girls," contains two parts: first part "Boarding Pupils," and second part "Day Pupils." The "second book," the third part, which I have not translated, contains the regulations for the religious community.

2. "Privilege and approval" were granted by the vicar-general and archbishop of Paris after the mother superiors of the two Parisian congregations had given their approval of the document. The date of the privilege and approval, May 4, 1652, gives us proof that the 1705 *Règlemens* is a reprinting of the original 1652 *Règlemens*. The *privilège du roi* that follows the vicar-general's approval and by which Louis XIV gives the Ursulines of Paris the perpetual right to publish books is dated July 1, 1651, and offers further proof that the 1705 text only differs from the 1652 original in the date of publication and the publishing house.

The Education of Girls

Boarding Pupils

CHAPTER ONE

The General Order of Classes

1. The Ursuline religious order has been founded principally for the instruction and upbringing of girls and is obliged by its constitutions to receive boarders into its monasteries. To carry out these obligations and to avoid the disorder and confusion that usually arise in a community made up of many people carrying out different tasks, everything must be well organized and the duties of the nuns charged with the education of boarders must be established in regulations. These regulations will enable all nuns to bring about excellent results in the girls entrusted to them without harming their own spiritual lives.

2. This is why in every monastery the boarders will be separated, according to their age and capacity, into as many classes as necessary. Class size should not exceed eighteen or twenty girls, although it may be necessary to have more in a class temporarily.

3. As much as possible, the living quarters for boarders should be separated from those of the nuns. In addition, each class of boarders will have its own private area where boarders can read, sew, etc., as well as an oratory where the class can pray to God at the times scheduled for prayer and the study of the catechism. If there is no available room that can serve as an oratory, the classroom itself will have an altar in the form of a large armoire whose

doors are opened when the girls say their prayers but otherwise closed, or, at the very least, the classroom will have something that serves as an altar, covered with a fitted cloth, and a religious painting above it.[3]

4. There will be bedrooms[4] for each class of boarders, in which girls will have separate beds, in accordance with the Ursuline constitution. All boarders will take their meals together in a common dining room, but every class will have its own table. Instruction in writing will also take place in the dining room.

5. As it is stated in the constitution, a General Mistress will have authority over all classes. Each class will have its own two mistresses, each of whom, in alternating weeks, will take the main responsibility for the class. In addition, there will be a mistress for needlework and another to teach arithmetic, counting, spelling, and reading handwritten documents.[5] One of these additional mistresses will be named by the Mother Superior to replace the Class Mistress and carry out her duties when a Class Mistress is sick, engaged in spiritual exercises, or otherwise prevented from being in the classroom. If there are few boarders in a class, or if the boarders are incapable of learning so many things because of their young age, there is no need of a mistress for needlework or of one for arithmetic and spelling. However, both of these mistresses can still teach any boarders in the lower classes capable of learning their subjects if the Mother Superior approves.

6. One or two nuns will be assigned to teach handwriting to all the classes. If there is only a single class, this handwriting mistress will also teach arithmetic and spelling if the Mother Superior does not object.

7. As will be specified below, other nuns will also be employed in the care of the boarders.

---

3. There is no indication of what could serve as an altar, but at the least, it would have been a small piece of furniture that could be easily covered.

4. Although the word *chambre* (bedroom) is used, the boarders did not have individual private rooms but, rather, shared a large space with beds separated by curtains, or what we might call a dormitory.

5. The *Règlemens* uses the term *jeter* (to throw) for simple arithmetical calculations because small objects, called *jetons* (in both French and English), were thrown or moved about for addition and subtraction.

CHAPTER TWO
The General Mistress⁶ of the Boarding School

1. The General Mistress of the boarding school, in addition to what is assigned to her in the constitution, will observe the following points.

2. She will do everything possible to support the authority that the Class Mistresses have over their boarders. To accomplish this, she will pay no heed to any complaints that pupils make against the mistresses, but rather she will try to make the boarders hold their teachers in great esteem. This is necessary if they are to profit from the mistresses' instruction. For this same reason, she will never admonish a Class Mistress in front of the boarders or show that she does not approve of the Class Mistress's actions through her facial expressions or demeanor. She will find time outside of the classroom to give the Class Mistresses any criticism she believes necessary, and she will do this gently and with charity. She will observe this same rule with all other nuns employed in the teaching or service of the boarders.

3. At some time before the three or four principal feast days of the year, she will go into the classrooms to exhort the boarders to prepare themselves for the feast day by practicing the virtues appropriate to their age and level of understanding, if she feels such visits are helpful. She can also do this in a general meeting, in which all boarders are assembled.

4. About every two months, she will go into every class to see if the boarders are advancing in reading and writing as well as in all of the subjects they are taught. She can give a small reward, such as a holy picture, *Agnus Dei*, or some other such thing, to girls who have made progress and reprimand those who have been negligent.⁷

5. Once or twice a year, she will require that the regulations for boarders be read to every class, and she will find out from the Class Mistresses how each class has satisfied this requirement.

6. In the *Règlemens*, the term *maîtresse* (mistress) is reserved for the choir nuns, the religious of high social status or wealth who alone were allowed to teach and hold positions of authority in the convent. Ursuline choir nuns professed solemn vows of poverty, chastity, obedience, and teaching.

7. "The name *Agnus Dei* has been given to certain discs of wax impressed with the figure of a lamb and blessed at stated seasons by the Pope. They are sometimes round, sometimes oval in diameter. The lamb usually bears a cross or flag, while figures of saints or the name and arms of the Pope are also commonly impressed on the reverse. The *Agnus Dei* may be worn suspended round the neck, or they may be preserved as objects of devotion" ("Agnus Dei," Catholic Encyclopedia, vol. A, accessed July 18, 2020, https://www.newadvent.org/cathen/01220a.htm).

6. If a class is too large, from time to time she can move some girls to a higher class, taking their age and ability into consideration, if the Mother Superior gives her permission to do so.

7. If one of the mistresses makes her aware that a boarder's behavior merits correction, she will go into the classroom and correct the girl in the manner determined beforehand by the Mother Superior. She will do so without anger, in a gentle manner, as the constitution requires. In the case of older boarders aged twelve or thirteen, she will not attempt to correct them without the Mother Superior's permission.

8. She will take care to learn from the Class Mistress each boarder's temperament, behavior, likes and dislikes, and the progress the girl is making in the acquisition of virtue, in catechism, and in all other subjects. She can thus speak knowledgeably to the girl's parents, if this is necessary.

9. When the Class Mistress asks permission for her pupils to receive communion, the General Mistress will consult the Mother Superior before giving her answer at least three days ahead of the feast day when they wish to take communion. She may allow the boarders to receive the sacrament on the four or five principal feast days of the year without conferring with the Mother Superior. She will also ask the Mother Superior's permission to allow those girls in the class who have not yet made their First Communion to go to Confession.

10. When there are boarders ready to make their First Communion, she will notify the Mother Superior so that the girls may be prepared in the prescribed manner.

11. Before a girl is admitted to the boarding school, the General Mistress will inquire about the girl's age, health, name, social rank, and the residence of her mother and father. If the girl is an orphan, the General Mistress will find out who is responsible for the girl as well as who is responsible for her living expenses in the convent and any other needs. She will obtain the name of someone who knows the girl personally and can assure her that the information requested above is accurate. She will carry out all inquiries as promptly as possible and report everything to the Mother Superior. If she is satisfied that she has received trustworthy answers and if there are no other impediments, she will ask the parents or relatives to bring the girl to the convent for an interview with the Mother Superior, as required by the constitution. She will also provide the parents with a memorandum listing everything the girl will need in the boarding school.

12. When parents bring their daughter to the convent to take up residence,

the General Mistress will inform the Mother Superior of the girl's arrival so that the Mother Superior can welcome the girl, if she wishes to do so. The General Mistress will ask the Mother Superior into which class she should place the girl. She will then accompany the girl to church to adore God and dedicate herself to Him. If the Mother Superior did not greet the girl upon her arrival, the General Mistress will accompany the girl to meet the Mother Superior after the girl has been to church. If this initial contact reveals no obstacle to the girl's admittance, she can stay in the boarding school if that is her parents' wish.

13. If any girl, whether or not she has an inheritance, is admitted to the boarding school by judicial order, or if parents ask that their daughter be admitted to the boarding school in order to preserve her from dangers to which her character makes her susceptible, the General Mistress will record the names and social ranks of the persons who have brought the girl to the convent.[8] She can thus be sure to release the girl only to these persons or to their legal proxy. She will also find out who is authorized to visit the girl while she is in the convent. The General Mistress will do exactly as these parents or guardians tell her, with all prudence and diligence, so that nothing that takes place in the convent goes against the wishes of the parents or guardians.

14. She will make certain that parents know they are not allowed to see boarders on feast days or Sundays and that the boarders may never spend the night outside of the convent. The boarders may have meals with their families, but only rarely. However, they can go out of the convent to see their mothers and fathers or guardians.

15. It is her duty to speak to the parents of boarders from time to time about the behavior and character of their daughters. She must be careful not to exaggerate faults lest she offend the parents or give the impression that the nuns do not truly hold the girls in deep affection. She will treat the parents with civility, kindness, and the modesty appropriate to nuns. She will avoid engaging in conversations on matters that have nothing to do with her official duties.

16. When she is in the parlor with visitors, she will keep her veil lowered

8. This paragraph indicates that not all girls entered the boarding schools willingly. Barbara B. Diefendorf notes that rebellious children could be sent to convents for a time (273), while Elizabeth Rapley states that some teaching convents accepted girls as young as three years old if they were orphans or had lost their mother and the father did not feel competent to care for them (623). See Diefendorf, "Give Us Back Our Children: Patriarchal Authority and Parental Consent to Religious Vocations in Early Counter-Reformation France," *Journal of Modern History* 68, no. 2 (June 1996): 265–307; and Elizabeth Rapley, "Women and Religious Vocation in Seventeenth-Century France," *French Historical Studies* 18 (1994): 613–31.

slightly over her face. When she opens the door of the reception room to allow boarders to leave the convent, she may not have her clothing hitched up. Her sleeves must be rolled down, and her small veil raised enough to be able to see and recognize the persons to whom she entrusts the girls. She will take care not to talk as long as the door is open, as the constitution requires.

17. Whenever a tailor or seamstress enters the convent to take measurements or try clothing on a boarder, the General Mistress will be present and accompanied by another nun. She will ensure the quality of the sewing. In the winter, she will have a fire lit in the room if the boarder must undress. Above all, she will keep an eye out for any letters or notes that might be given to a boarder during these times. To do this, she will always have her veil raised above her eyes. She will arrange things so that a tailor or seamstress never comes back more than twice to fit a single article of clothing.

18. She will take care that nothing is given in secret to a boarder in the reception room, especially books. She will not tolerate any books that do not inspire piety. For this reason, the boarders must show her any books they have been given. If these are not pious books, the General Mistress will send them back to the donor. She will also show any books on piety that are not already in the convent to the Mother Superior. The only ones she will allow the boarders to keep are those that are clearly spiritual and appropriate to nuns or others well advanced in the spiritual life.

19. She will inform the Bursar when any of a boarder's clothes are returned to her family, just as she will inform the Linen Mistress when any linen is returned. She will also inform them whenever any new clothing or linen comes into the convent.

20. Every year at the onset of winter, she will inspect the boarders' clothing to make sure that they have sufficient clothing to stay warm. If they lack anything, she will let the parents know what they need. She will remove any clothing that a boarder can no longer use and ask the Bursar to store it, or she can store it herself if she has a place to do so. She will give the clothing back to the parents if they ask for it or when the girl leaves the convent. It is a good idea for her to perform the same inspection at the beginning of the summer.

21. She will not allow the boarders to give money or anything else to help with the class's expenses for needlework or to decorate the class oratory unless the girl's parents have approved the donation.

22. When a boarder wishes to have masses said or to give money to the poor, the General Mistress will see that the money for such purposes is given

to the Bursar and indicate to whom the money should be distributed, always following the Mother Superior's will and the boarder's intentions. She may also decide to have the poor come into the reception room so that the boarders themselves can distribute the money. The same rule applies for old clothes or linen that parents wish to distribute to the poor.

23. She will provide Class Mistresses that need them books on Christian doctrine, such as the *Roman Catechism*, the great treasury of writings on Christian doctrine, Cardinal Richelieu's *L'Instruction du Chrétien*, etc.[9] When they are no longer necessary for class preparation, Class Mistresses will take care to return those books that have been lent to them.

24. With the Mother Superior's permission, every year the General Mistress will take from the class funds (these funds consist of money donated for needlework expenses, oratory decorations, and the sale of bits of candle left over from *La Chandeleur*)[10] the amount necessary for class prizes. This sum should never exceed 40 or 50 *sols* per class.[11] After the Bursar has bought what is needed, the General Mistress will distribute the money to each Class Mistress, giving her the amount deducted from the funds of her class. The General Mistress may also take one *écu* per girl from the boarding school's general fund and use this money for prizes.[12] Such withdrawals of money should be done only where it is easy to do so. Otherwise, the Mother Superior will decide where the money for prizes should be obtained, or she may decide to find other ways of rewarding the classes.

25. She will make no important innovations or changes to the established class schedule without the Mother Superior's permission, nor will she authorize any expensive needlework, such as altar decorations, without the Mother Superior's permission.

26. Normally she will take her meals in the same dining room as the boarders but at a separate table at the far end of the room. She does this to ensure that the boarders behave as they should but also to ensure that those who serve the meals do so correctly. If there are only a few boarders in the con-

9. The *Roman Catechism* is the official catechism commissioned by the Council of Trent and published in 1566. The "grand trésor de doctrine chrétienne" mentioned here does not refer to a specific book. *L'Instruction du Chrétien* was written and published by Cardinal Richelieu, minister of Louis XIII, in 1642.

10. Candlemas, the French celebration of the Feast of the Purification of the Virgin, is always held on February 2.

11. *Sol* is the early spelling of *sou*, a small sum of money perhaps equivalent to today's "cent."

12. Equivalent to today's euro.

vent, she need only go to the dining room from time to time. Before the food is brought to the boarders' table, she will check the plates to verify both the quantity and the quality of the food being served. If anything is lacking, she will notify the Mother Superior.

27. If at all possible, her bedroom will be close to the boarders' dormitory. This will enable her to take care of any unexpected problem during the night.

28. When a boarder falls sick, the General Mistress will explain the nature of the illness to the Mother Superior and the nurse so they can care for the girl properly. Once the girl is in the infirmary, the General Mistress will visit her occasionally to learn about her condition and medical treatment. She will also inform the parents of their daughter's illness. When the illness is of long duration, she will ask the parents to take the girl home until she recovers, if it is possible to do so easily and if the Mother Superior and the doctor advise such a move.

29. If a boarder expresses to the General Mistress her wish to become an Ursuline nun in the convent where she resides, and if the girl is old enough to act upon her wish, the General Mistress will discuss the matter with the Mother Superior.[13] If the Mother Superior approves of this wish, the General Mistress will take the girl to her room and explain beforehand the *Regulations of the Ursuline Order* found in the third book.[14] If the girl is not sure of her vocation, the General Mistress should consult both the Mother Superior and certain Class Mistresses to determine whether the girl should be required to spend some time away from the convent before entering the novitiate. If it is judged appropriate for the girl to return to the world in order to test and

13. According to Diefendorf, the legal age of maturity for both men and women in the seventeenth century was twenty-five, well beyond the age when boarders had finished their education in the Ursuline schools. The Catholic Church, however, had officially adopted the position elaborated by the Council of Trent that sixteen was the age of "perfect reason" for undertaking the decision to enter the religious life (Diefendorf, 285–86). When the *Règlemens* states that a girl must be "old enough to act upon her wish," it seems to refer to girls who are not younger than sixteen and nearing the end of their studies. Although there is no mention made of parental approval, the previous paragraphs treating the need for parental approval before a girl is accepted in the *pensionnat* suggest that the Ursulines would have been unwilling to accept as a novice any girl whose parents had strong objections. Diefendorf notes further that while in the early years of the Counter-Reformation, parents often did object to their children entering the highly ascetic orders, such as the Discalced Carmelites, that separated their children forever from the world, after 1630 they were less likely to object to girls entering the teaching orders, especially the Ursulines, which were much less ascetic (306).

14. The third book refers to the second part of the 1705 *Règlemens*, entitled "Des Règlemens communs du monastère," which gives the nuns' daily schedule, both for devotional practices and teaching. Several chapters deal with the proper comportment of novices toward the mother superior. This part disappears from the 1861 *Règlements*.

reaffirm her intention of entering religious life, or even to help her understand if she has a true inclination to enter religious life, the girl may not be promised a place in the novitiate before she leaves the convent. The girl will thus enjoy complete freedom in her decision.

CHAPTER THREE

The Class Mistresses

1. Having been chosen for a task as important as the education of girls and wishing to carry it out as perfectly as possible, the Class Mistresses should, before all else, ask our Savior to guide them spiritually in such a holy enterprise. Then they should give themselves over to their work with great affection and a heart filled with charity and zeal, trying to form themselves in the true spirit of the Ursuline order, which is so well expressed in the first part of the Ursuline constitution. To this end, they should read the constitution often.

2. For the benefit of the boarders, they should apply themselves to developing a behavior filled with kindness and charity, prudence and discretion, and a maternal foresight that is full of goodness and is neither too anxious nor too critical.

3. The older of the two Class Mistresses has the main responsibility for the class and is known as the First Class Mistress. This responsibility consists above all in teaching the girls to turn fully to God and to offer themselves to Him with all their heart. As it is written in the constitution, they must teach girls to confess their sins properly, to receive communion, to listen devoutly at mass, and to engage in other pious exercises that are useful in overcoming passions and bad inclinations. The mistress should help girls recognize which passions are strongest in them. She should give them some exercise in virtue appropriate to each girl's needs, age, and ability to understand and teach her to meditate on the life, death, and Passion of our Lord as well as on other mysteries of our faith they are capable of understanding. She will speak to the girls individually from time to time about the points listed above.

4. The boarders should address their requests to receive Holy Communion or for permissions in other important matters to this same mistress.

5. In all other matters concerning the instruction and care of the boarders, the two mistresses will observe the following weekly schedule:

6. The mistress who is *en semaine* must be with the boarders during class time.[15] The other must be present at choir and attend all other regular devotional observances, including vespers and matins, beginning with the Saturday she finishes her week *en semaine*.[16]

7. Both mistresses will be present in the dormitory in the morning when the boarders awaken to comb their hair and, if necessary, dress them and arrange their hair. Once they have done this, the mistress who is *en semaine* may leave, and the other mistress will stay in the dormitory until fifteen minutes before mass begins. She will make sure that the girls are properly dressed and groomed, have taken care of their needs,[17] washed their mouths and hands and taken their handkerchiefs, head coverings, gloves, etc., with them before they leave the dormitory.

8. If there are two dormitories for a single class, each of the two class mistresses will take charge of one dormitory. If it is possible, a replacement mistress will stay in the dormitory when it is time for the mistress who is *en semaine* to leave.

9. The mistress *en semaine* will accompany the boarders to the class oratory to say their prayers and then to mass. She will remain close to them during mass to see that they maintain proper reverence. Once mass is over, she will conduct them to class. One half-hour later, she will lead them in prayer to call them to attention and begin the lessons of reading, needlework, etc. Fifteen minutes later, after the other mistress has arrived, she may leave the class for thirty minutes or three-quarters of an hour at the very most. The mistress *en semaine* will lead the boarders in their recitation of litanies at the appointed time. She will take them to the dining room from the classroom and dine with them at the far end of their table and stay with them during recess, after which she will resume lessons as in the morning. Sometime after readings have taken place among the religious community, the mistress who is not *en semaine* will come into the classroom. If the boarders do not have writing lessons after the midday meal, this mistress may go say vespers at 1:45 p.m., or do something else, and be back in the classroom at 2:15. At 3:00 p.m., she will leave to go say her prayers, and the mistress *en semaine* will stay in the classroom until 4:00 p.m.

15. The Ursulines used a system of teaching that allowed the two teachers to take turns being the lead teacher. The term *en semaine* refers to the lead teacher, that is, the one who has primary responsibility for the week.

16. Vespers is the service of evening prayer and matins the service of morning prayer.

17. Go to the bathroom.

10. The Class Mistress will teach catechism at the appointed time, eat the evening meal with the boarders and, after recess, listen to them say their prayers and make their examination of conscience. Once they are all in bed and the nun who stays with them during the night has arrived, she may leave the dormitory. If there are two dormitories, the replacement for the mistress *en semaine*, as well as another nun appointed for that week, will be present in one of the dormitories while the girls undress for bed.

11. The mistress *en semaine* will accompany her girls to the dining room when it is time for the writing lesson. She will lead them in a prayer if they have not already said one and then leave them with the writing teacher. At the end of the lesson, she will return to the dining room and accompany them back to their classroom.

12. The Class Mistresses, with the permission of the Mother Superior and the General Mistress, may change the time when their boarders have the writing lesson from the morning to the afternoon.

13. On Sundays and feast days, in those convents where a low mass is said before the high mass, the mistress who is not *en semaine* will attend low mass with the boarders. If a sermon is preached either before or after vespers, she will stay with the boarders for an hour to give the priest enough time to complete his sermon. The mistress who is *en semaine* will stay with the boarders the rest of the day. This does not preclude the possibility of the mistress *en semaine* getting help from the other mistress if the two mistresses decide such an arrangement better suits their needs.

14. During the time the boarders are in the classroom, the Class Mistress will sit next to them and have them read aloud one after the other. Or she may use the following method.

15. Each girl will have her own book and all will be seated in rows, with the mistress in front of them. The mistress and the boarders will make the Sign of the Cross. Then the mistress will read aloud five or six lines slowly, emphasizing each word.[18] After this, she will read one or two pages with a clear pronunciation, making the appropriate pauses in her sentences and accenting the necessary words. The boarders will have their eyes on their books and follow what the mistress is reading, repeating what she reads word for word in a low voice. At the conclusion of this reading, the mistress

---

18. The *Règlemens* uses the word *épeler*, which in modern French means "to spell" but which in the seventeenth century had the meaning of pronouncing slowly and distinctly.

will choose one girl to read all or part of the text aloud, then another, until the whole class has read aloud. The mistress will correct the girls when they make mistakes.

16. The reading lesson will take place twice a day, in the morning and the afternoon, once in Latin and once in French. The General Mistress will designate the times for reading lessons. Each of the mistresses will teach one of the lessons.

17. In the lower classes, where younger boarders are usually less able to read, the lesson should be shorter and the mistress should repeat the lesson several times if needed. Those girls who cannot yet read in French will read twice a day in Latin.

18. The Mother Superior will decide which of these two methods will be used to teach reading.[19] She will base her choice on the method that experience has proven best suited to teach her boarders.

19. In classes that use the latter method of teaching reading, the mistresses will, when the lesson is finished, take a few of the slowest girls aside and have them read in a leisurely fashion. The Class Mistresses will also examine the girls' needlework from time to time. They may ask the girls to read sometimes during their writing lesson or ask them to count and do arithmetic during this time to understand better what they know and to have an opportunity to encourage them to learn well.

20. Once a week the mistresses will accompany the boarders to the Linen Mistress's quarters to fold their personal linen. Each class will go separately on different days and at different times, such as after vespers or some other suitable moment. The Class Mistress will remain with the boarders until they have finished their work. If the Class Mistresses decide it is easier to have the boarders fold their linen in the classroom, they will ensure that the linen is folded properly and that the boarders then store the linen immediately in their trunks.

21. The Class Mistresses will not change the prescribed schedule of lessons. They may only change the schedule with the permission of the Mother Superior and the General Mistress. They may also not change the type of prayers or the wording of the prayers the boarders say.

22. The Class Mistress will urge the girls to observe the Regulations for the Boarders.[20] This is necessary if the girls are to become what they should be

19. All classes in the convent would then use the same method.
20. These regulations are found in chapter fifteen, "Regulations for the Boarders."

and what their parents wish them to be. In order to accomplish this, in addition to the General Mistress's reading of the regulations, the Class Mistresses will read the regulations with the boarders once or twice to make them aware of their failures and encourage them to try harder.

23. Class Mistresses should take great care to assist the boarders in becoming pious and devout. They must teach them to be virtuous Christians and train them in prayer and those inner acts of virtue of which they are capable. The mistresses will sometimes give the boarders ideas for their prayers or have them find ideas in books, especially on the days when the boarders receive Holy Communion but more often if they benefit from this practice. The mistresses will also give the boarders books on piety that they are capable of understanding so they can become accustomed to reading good books and profiting from them. Every classroom will have a number of such books available, and the mistresses will care for the books.

24. Mistresses will devote themselves to forming boarders who are polite and agreeable,[21] who speak correctly, have good posture and act courteously, put the needs of others before their own, and always treat the nuns with respect.

25. They should train the boarders to become good wives, to care for their clothing, to always be clean, and to pay attention to any task they are given. From time to time, they should show the boarders how to mend the clothing that has been ripped or if a seam has come undone. They may not permit the boarders to modify clothes, give away any clothes, or cut up their old clothes without the General Mistress's permission.

26. The boarders' good health is the mistress's greatest responsibility. Therefore, she will do nothing that might affect their health, nor will she use any form of punishment, such as deprive them of food or expose them to the cold, that could make them sick. She will always be attentive to the boarders' physical needs, giving them whatever is required to relieve their discomfort or, if she herself does not have the means to do so, procuring what is required. If a boarder falls ill, she will inform the General Mistress.

27. During recess, she will do everything possible to keep all the girls in her class together, so she can watch over them and observe how they act. She will maintain a happy and calm demeanor, taking care, nevertheless, not to

21. The *Règlemens* uses the term *honnête*, which in the seventeenth century did not mean "honest" but, rather, "unpedantic, sociable, modest, and polite," as in Pascal's treatment of *l'honnête homme* in *Pensées*.

become too friendly with the girls or to converse with them about useless and silly things. She will never discuss with them the nuns' penitential practices or any other of the nuns' practices. She will not tolerate any disparagement of a nun or of anyone else.

28. She must keep the boarders cheerful and happy, teach them how to play simple games and take part in them herself. She will never permit anything indecent, like acting, dancing, card games, or other such things. Nor should she allow boarders to sing bad songs, such as those with slanderous lyrics, etc.

29. She will maintain a spirit of unity among all the boarders in her class and will teach them to treat each other most charitably. To create this common spirit, she herself will treat all of the boarders in the same way and act charitably even toward those boarders who are unpleasant or not very intelligent or otherwise lacking in qualities.

30. She must never discourage the boarders but rather inspire them to study better and to become more virtuous through her example. She must show them how much their slightest progress pleases her and praise them from time to time. She should give little presents, like holy pictures, or *Agnus Dei*, to those boarders who have done their best, especially in the lower classes.

31. Every two months or so, she will make a list for the Bursar of everything the boarders need and give it to the General Mistress.

32. When a boarder in an upper class has the General Mistress's permission to donate money for the class's needlework expenses or to decorate the class oratory, the Class Mistress will designate an older girl from the class to keep the money. When it comes time to use the money, the Class Mistress will make a list of the necessary purchases and give it to the General Mistress. The Bursar will keep any money donated from the lower classes, and the Class Mistress will write down the amount donated to ensure it is used properly, according to the General Mistress's authorization.

33. If a boarder wishes to make a gift to the Class Mistress, the Mother Superior must give her permission before the Class Mistress can accept anything. The Class Mistress may never express a desire for a gift, even if she intends to give it in alms to the poor.

34. The Class Mistresses will respect each other and learn to work together in a unified and charitable way. They must be of one mind in their

dealings with the boarders. The Class Mistress who is not *en semaine* will defer to the Class Mistress *en semaine*, while this latter mistress will defer to the General Mistress.

35. The two Class Mistresses will discuss with each other all matters pertaining to the management of the class, and they will do so during their time outside of the classroom when no boarders are present. From time to time, the First Class Mistress will give an accounting of the boarders' temperament, their behavior, health, etc., to the General Mistress. The Second Class Mistress may also give her own accounting if the General Mistress questions her.

36. The Class Mistresses will never discuss their boarders' faults with other Class Mistresses or with any other nuns in their convent, unless such discussions may prove useful for the boarders' well-being. They must never reveal what a boarder has told them in confidence.

37. Should a boarder move to a different class, the Class Mistresses of the original class will no longer have any authority over her. All authority will be given to the Class Mistress who is currently in charge.

38. The First Class Mistress will confer authority to the Second Class Mistress and do everything possible so that the boarders recognize the authority of the Second Class Mistress and respect and obey her. In this regard, the Second Class Mistress should be in the classroom during the reading of the regulations for boarders and whenever the General Mistress comes into the classroom to inquire about the boarders' actions so that she can give her own observations of the boarders' behavior. The First Mistress will never take a boarder aside and ask questions about the Second Mistress's actions or behavior. She will never listen to the boarders' complaints about the Second Mistress with obvious pleasure nor allow any inappropriate remarks. The Second Mistress will follow the exact same conduct with respect to the First Mistress.

39. The two Class Mistresses must never allow the boarders to witness any little disagreement that may arise between them, or any disagreements with the General Mistress, or see that the mistresses disapprove of each other's actions. If one does find fault with the other, she should let her know about this after class and do so kindly and charitably.

40. The Class Mistresses will observe the same behavior with all the other teachers who come into their classrooms and with all other nuns who serve the

boarders. At the same time, the Class Mistresses should keep an eye on these other nuns to ensure that they perform their duties correctly and diligently.

41. Above all, the Class Mistresses will take care to demonstrate to the boarders the high esteem in which they hold all nuns. They will not allow the boarders to speak badly of nuns, whether an individual nun or nuns in general. The mistresses will be especially careful not to engage in such conversation when it concerns those Class Mistresses who have taught the boarders in earlier years. They will refrain from finding any fault with the conduct of former mistresses or show any curiosity about their conduct.

42. If a boarder expresses the desire to become a nun, the Class Mistresses will tell her to pray to God about her vocation, as this is the most important step she can take. They will use this opportunity to encourage the boarder to become more virtuous and to correct any fault that could keep her from such great happiness. They will advise her to keep her plans secret until it is appropriate to declare them. They, too, will keep this secret.

43. When a girl has reached the age when she can declare her intentions and she has persisted in her resolve to become a nun in the convent where she resides, the First Class Mistress will notify the Mother Superior and the General Mistress, and the three of them together will decide if it is proper for her to seek admission to the order. If they deem it proper, the Class Mistress will arrange for the girl herself to express her desires to the General Mistress so that the General Mistress can direct her. If the girl wishes to join another order or join a different convent, the Mother Superior, General Mistress, and the First Class Mistress will give her the best possible advice, both for the greater glory of God and for the girl's own spiritual well-being.

44. If a girl is obviously unfit for the Ursuline order, the Class Mistresses must gently persuade her that this is not the right religious order for her and help her choose a more suitable convent. Or, without saying anything else, they can encourage the girl in general terms to consider the religious life. They must then notify the Mother Superior, who, if the girl's age is such that the matter requires urgent attention, can suggest that the parents take the girl out of the boarding school.

45. The Class Mistresses may not dispose of anything that belongs to their classrooms and oratories, such as decorations, pictures, etc. They may not give these things away, damage them, or change them in any way without the permission of the General Mistress.

CHAPTER FOUR
How the Mistresses Must Instruct the Boarders in Piety

I.

Catechism

1. Before beginning the catechism lesson, the mistresses will prepare the subject matter in order to understand its meaning and its importance. The mistress should ask the Holy Spirit for grace and enlightenment to do this.

2. At the beginning of the class, when all the boarders are seated, the mistress makes the Sign of the Cross, as do the boarders. The girl who has been appointed by the mistress will stand next to the mistress and begin reading the catechism text. She then asks questions of a classmate, who stands when answering. The mistress allows the classmate to sit after she has answered one or two questions. The class proceeds in this way for about fifteen minutes until the entire class, or part of the class, answers. It is important to have the girls speak distinctly and calmly. From time to time, the questions should not simply be factual but require an understanding of the text. If a girl cannot answer a question, the mistress should give her the answer.

3. There follows a review of the preceding day's catechism lesson conducted through questions and answers. The mistress should change the wording of the questions to help the boarders strengthen their knowledge of what they have been taught and not only retain the subject but truly understand what they have memorized. It is a good idea to begin by questioning those girls who are the least knowledgeable and, if they cannot answer, to turn then to those who are more knowledgeable. If the mistress sees that neither group has retained anything, or very little, of the preceding day's catechism, she should repeat the previous lesson and not teach anything new that day.

4. Once the review of the previous day's lesson has taken place, the mistress proceeds with the catechism lesson introduced at the beginning of the hour. She should address the subject clearly, distinctly, and briefly and explain it, as much as possible, through stories. Stories are especially useful for teaching those boarders who do not know the catechism well or have difficulty understanding it. For those parts of the catechism that cannot be taught through stories, such as the Theological Virtues[22] or the sacraments,

---

22. Faith, hope, and charity.

THREE CENTURIES OF GIRLS' EDUCATION

the mistress should use comparisons with familiar things that the boarders are capable of understanding.

5. After the explanation, the mistress will find it useful to arouse in the boarders those sentiments connected to the day's catechism lesson. If the subject is the Creation, she should encourage them to thank God for having made them for such a noble purpose and for having given them a soul capable of loving Him and of enjoying eternal happiness with Him. If it is the four final ends,[23] she should inspire them to fear God and his judgment by telling them a suitable story. If they are talking about the mystery of the Redemption, she should incite them to love our Savior Jesus Christ and teach them, especially the older boarders, how to make the acts of Faith, Hope, and Charity and to pray fervently. By giving them the example of a saint or telling them a story, she will quicken their desire to practice what they have been learning.

6. It is good for the boarders to ask questions, but the questions should be related to the subject being addressed. Otherwise, they are a waste of time.

7. The divine mysteries must be treated with respect. The mistress should speak without haste and have her wits about her when she speaks. She can use a book or other text as an aid for her memory.

8. She will not go beyond the time allotted for catechism class, that is, about three-quarters of an hour. The class is over when the bell rings.

9. As they prepare the catechism lesson, the mistresses may use the *Roman Catechism*, Cardinal Richelieu's *de l'Instruction du Chrétien*, the works of Bellarmine, Father Bonnefons,[24] etc. They should not feel obliged to use the exact words or organization of these books. Rather, they should take from them only what they find helpful and what the boarders are capable of understanding.

II.

How to Prepare Boarders for the Sacrament of Confession

1. When the time has come for those boarders who have not yet made their First Communion to go to confession, that is, every six weeks or two

---

23. Death, judgment, hell, and heaven.

24. Saint Robert Bellarmine (1542–1621) was an Italian Jesuit and cardinal who wrote widely on matters of Christian doctrine but also devotional works in Latin, such as *The Art of Dying Well* (1619). He was declared a Doctor of the Church in 1931. Amable Bonnefons was a Jesuit and a devotional writer of the second half of the sixteenth century. He wrote works used in catechizing children, such as *Abrégé de la doctrine chrestienne* (The Concise Christian Doctrine [1548]).

months for the little girls between six and eight years old and once a month for all other girls, the First Class Mistress will notify the General Mistress, who will decide upon the day for confession.

2. A few days before, if she deems it necessary, the mistress *en semaine* will review the parts of the catechism dealing with the sacrament of Penance. She will explain the three stages of Penance—contrition, confession, and satisfaction—and help the girls understand the necessity of making a full confession. She will teach them how to confess correctly and how to examine their conscience beforehand. During this review, she should emphasize any one of the three stages of Penance she feels is important.

3. On the day when the boarders are to go to confession, one of the mistresses should give them a short prayer inspired by the Passion of Our Lord or some other subject that will cause them to feel sorrow for their sins. The boarders can meditate on this subject during mass. If time permits, the mistress can then help the boarders compose their own acts of contrition. She should calmly recite a model act of contrition, which the boarders can repeat silently.

4. At the appointed time, the First Mistress will accompany a group of boarders to church. Before they enter the confessional, the mistress will speak to each girl individually in a quiet place and help her examine her conscience for the sins she has committed since her last confession. To simplify the examination of conscience, the mistress should ask the boarder to consider three categories: sins against God, her neighbor, and herself, whether in thought, word, or deed. The mistress should ask the girls, especially, to examine any inclinations toward sin that she herself has noticed in them. She should encourage them once again to be contrite and to resolve to sin no more. If necessary, she should review with them the proper way to make their confession.

5. She must take great care, when helping a boarder with the examination of conscience, to be judicious and discreet and not ask any questions that could suggest sinful matters the girl knows nothing about. At the same time, the mistress should give the girl every opportunity to address any sins she has committed.

6. To save time, the mistress may also have the boarders make their examination of conscience together in the class oratory and excuse those boarders who already know how to do so.

7. The mistress will make certain that there is always someone prepared to make her confession so the confessor never has to wait.

III.

Communion

1. Having learned from the General Mistress which boarders are to receive communion, the First Class Mistress will contact those girls a few days before and urge them to prepare themselves for the sacrament. She can read them a passage from the catechism or some other book that explains how to prepare for communion and also lists the intentions one should have and the benefits obtained from communion when it is made properly. She should encourage them to prepare themselves by performing virtuous acts, both exterior and interior.

2. As noted above, on the preceding day, the First Mistress will give the boarders a short prayer to guide them in confessing their sins. It is not necessary to help each girl individually make an examination of conscience since these boarders know what to do. Nevertheless, if a boarder needs help, the First Mistress should assist her, following the method given in the paragraphs on confession.

3. Thirty minutes before mass on the day when these boarders are to receive communion, the First Mistress should give the boarders a short meditation on the life of the saint whose feast is being celebrated that day, applying in some way lessons from the life of that saint to the reception of the sacrament. The girls should go to church to pray fifteen minutes before mass begins.

4. The rest of that day, the mistress will help the girls who have taken the sacrament maintain an attitude of modesty and calm as they think about the benefits they have just received.

5. At 4:45 in the afternoon, she will accompany them to church for fifteen minutes of prayer. If there is no sermon during the afternoon service, she can give the girls beforehand some spiritual reading on which they can meditate.

IV.

How to Instruct Boarders Preparing
for the Sacrament of Confirmation

1. Having learned the date when the sacrament of Confirmation is to be conferred, the mistresses will instruct the boarders ahead of time, questioning them on why this sacrament was instituted, the form the sacrament takes, its substance and effects, and the reason for the ceremonies with which it

is conferred. The boarders should understand why the bishop confers this sacrament, the dispositions they should bring to it, and why they can only be confirmed once in a lifetime.

2. The preceding day, the mistress will have the boarders go to confession. The morning when they are to be confirmed, she will remind them of the principal instructions she has given them regarding Confirmation, and she will exhort them to receive the sacrament with great reverence and devotion.

3. Each girl must have her headband ready to give to whoever will place it on her forehead during the ceremony. Later that evening, the girls will return to church to have the headband removed, as it is specified in the *Ceremonial Procedures of the Divine Office*.[25]

V.

How to Teach the Boarders to Offer Themselves to God

1. Once a girl has been admitted to the boarding school, the mistress makes her aware of her obligation to serve God and to love Him henceforth with all her heart, not only because He created the world but also because He has redeemed it and adopted the girl as one of His children. The mistress will encourage the girl to offer herself completely to God and to renew the vows made on her behalf when she was baptized. The mistress should use the following prayer, which contains acts of faith, adoration, thanksgiving, contrition, offering, and petition.

2. Act of Faith and Adoration: "Almighty and Eternal God, I prostrate myself before your adorable and infinite majesty. I recognize and proclaim you as my God, my Creator, and my sovereign Lord, and I adore you in all humility."

Act of Thanksgiving: "Recognizing the favors you have bestowed on me in your infinite goodness, I thank you most humbly, especially for having created me in your image and likeness; for giving me a soul capable of knowing, loving, and serving you so I can be eternally happy with you; for redeeming

25. As early as the thirteenth century, the churches in Ireland and England required that children bring "fillets or bands of sufficient length and width" for the ceremony of Confirmation and that the same children must be brought to the church the third day after Confirmation to have their foreheads washed by the priest out of reverence for the holy chrism. See "Confirmation," *Catholic Encyclopedia*, vol. C, accessed April 12, 2020, newadvent.org/cathen/04215b.htm. The title "Ceremonial Procedures of the Divine Office" refers to the description of liturgical observances written by and for the Ursuline Nuns of the Congregation of Paris.

me by the precious blood of your only Son; for calling me to the true faith and bestowing on me the fruits of the Redemption through Baptism and all the other sacraments; for preserving me, since the moment of my birth, from a multitude of evils, both spiritual and physical, and granting me so many good things and graces."

Act of Contrition: "I confess, Oh, my God, that I was already obliged to love and serve you when I took my first breath and yet, until now, I have lived without honoring and serving you as I must, and, what is worse, I have offended you in so many ways. I ask you to forgive me most humbly and with my sincere regrets."

Offering: "I beg you with all my heart to accept the offer of my whole being, of my life, my thoughts, my words, and my deeds. In the presence of your Divine Majesty, I renew the promises made for me at my baptism to renounce Satan and all his works, as well as the pomp and vanities of this world. I declare that I would prefer to die a thousand deaths rather than separate myself, even for a moment, from my faith or the observance of your holy commandments, in obedience to which I resolve to live and to die. I humbly beg you for the grace to keep these promises through the merits of your Son, whom you love so well, and by the intercession of the glorious Virgin, my guardian angel, and all my patron saints. Amen."

CHAPTER FIVE

How to Prepare Boarders to Make Their First Communion

I.

1. The date chosen for the First Communion of those boarders who are ready to receive the sacrament will be one of the principal feast days of the year, that is, Easter, Pentecost, Assumption of the Blessed Virgin Mary, All Saints' Day, or Christmas.

2. Seven weeks beforehand, the General Mistress will consult individually with the Class Mistresses to determine which girls are ready to make their First Communion. She will ask their ages, their ability to understand and judge well, and especially about their morals. She will then make a list of their names, give the list to the Mother Superior, and tell her the reasons for proposing these girls.

3. After the Mother Superior has decided which girls will receive the sacrament, the General Mistress will go into each class. She will first invoke the inspiration of the Holy Spirit, then speak for a short time about the importance of making a worthy communion, after which she will announce the names of the boarders who have been chosen. She will speak to these girls briefly about their great good fortune, about the esteem in which they should hold the honor they have been given, and about the fervor they should bring to preparing themselves for this honor. She will then entrust them to the First Class Mistress, who will teach and prepare them for the next six weeks, using the method explained in the following paragraph, unless the Mother Superior herself has deemed it appropriate to undertake the work of preparing the boarders.

4. Those boarders who have already made their First Communion before coming to the convent should be put with those who are being prepared, as much to refresh their knowledge of the catechism as to teach them, if necessary, how to make a general confession.

II.
How to Prepare for First Communion

1. Instruction should take place in a different room than the regular classroom. Every day, the mistress should find a suitable hour to teach catechism to those preparing for First Communion.

2. She will use the method to teach catechism explained above, except that the text will not be read aloud and the day's subject will be studied more briefly.[26] The mistress will place more importance on developing pious and virtuous girls than on memorization. Although both knowledge and virtue are necessary, devotion and virtue are of greater value to the girls and more pleasing to God than knowledge.

3. When she is ready to begin the preparation, the mistress will first bring the girls to church so they can offer themselves to our Lord, asking for the grace to benefit from what they are about to learn in order to become worthy of the sacrament. To this end, they should implore first the assistance of the

26. This is a reference to chapter four, section I, "How to Teach Catechism." The mistresses assume that boarders who are ready to make their First Communion already know and understand the elements of Catholic doctrine that qualify them to receive the sacrament with consent. Thus, the mistresses place less importance on memorization and analysis than on the formation of the will.

Holy Virgin, then of their guardian angel and the saint they have chosen to guide their preparation. Every day before catechism, they will repeat these prayers in the same room where instruction takes place.

4. Beginning with the first catechism lesson, the mistress will make sure the girls understand the reason for this preparation, which is to make them worthy of becoming living temples of God the Son, who will enter into each of them personally. She will do her best to have them hold this sacrament in the highest esteem. She must instill in them a great desire to prepare themselves fully as well as a fear of approaching the sacrament unworthily.

5. The mistress will then touch briefly upon the idea that communion, if it is to be received worthily, requires a twofold preparation. The preparation of lesser importance requires a thorough understanding of the four principal parts of Christian doctrine: first, Faith, which is set forth in the Apostles' Creed; second, Hope, presented in the Lord's Prayer; third, Charity, proclaimed in the Ten Commandments; fourth, reception of the sacraments, especially Penance and the Eucharist.

6. The other preparation, which is more important and of more immediate concern, requires a purity of conscience obtained through a well-made general confession and the practice of virtue and good works. The mistress must help the boarders understand the necessity of a pure conscience. She will teach them to prepare their souls by making acts, both spoken and silent, of faith, hope, charity, devotion, humility, and purity of heart and of intention, out of a desire to receive our Lord. Every week, the mistress will give them one of these prayers to practice, explaining how to behave while praying. From time to time, she will ask them to give an account of their behavior.

7. If the General Mistress approves, the Class Mistress may have the girls practice some special devotion, such as going to vespers and matins, or spending fifteen minutes in prayer, etc. Nevertheless, she must be careful not to overburden the girls, lest they grow weary of too much preparation and find it distasteful.

III.

Parts of Christian Doctrine They Must Teach

1. After she has presented the four principal parts of Christian doctrine treated in paragraph 5 of the preceding article, the mistress will explain each of these parts one at a time.

2. She will first address Faith. She will explain what is meant by Faith, why Faith is a theological virtue, its aim, its effects, when it is given to us, and how we should practice it. Then she will explain, in detail, the Apostles' Creed, which contains the expression of our faith.

3. From there, she will move on to the second virtue, Hope, and will follow the same order of explanation as with Faith.

4. She will then speak to the boarders about Charity in the same way. She will also explain the First Commandment, reserving her study of the other commandments for general confession.

5. She will give them the general definition of a sacrament. She will tell them how many sacraments there are, which ones are necessary for our salvation, who instituted them and for what end. Then she will speak to them briefly about Baptism, Confirmation, and Penance, putting aside a discussion of the other sacraments[27] for another time so that she can spend more time on the Holy Sacrament of the Altar,[28] which is the main subject.

6. She will insist upon the excellence of this sacrament, which surpasses the value of all the others, because this sacrament contains in itself the author of all the sacraments. She will make it clear that they must believe in Christ's real presence in this sacrament and explain to them how our Lord is present there, both as man and as God. She must talk about the miracle that takes place in the Eucharist, the effects the sacrament produces in the souls of those prepared to receive it, the reason for the sacrament's institution, etc.

7. The mistress has the discretion to omit any part of the aforementioned catechism that she knows is too difficult for her boarders to understand as long as she teaches them the essential points. She should feel free to do this especially if she notes that her boarders are not very intelligent or if they are close-minded but must be prepared for First Communion because of their age or some other circumstance.

8. At the end of these four weeks spent studying Christian doctrine, the mistress will summon the Father Superior of the convent school or, in his absence, the Confessor, to question the boarders on what they have studied. If he judges some girls insufficiently prepared, they will not be allowed to proceed and their First Communion will be postponed to a later date. Those he judges ready will proceed to preparation for confession.

27. Matrimony, Holy Orders, and Last Rites.
28. The Eucharist.

IV.

When and How to Prepare the Boarders for General Confession

1. The fifth week is spent preparing the boarders to make their General Confession. The mistress should make the boarders understand, above all, the utility, necessity, and importance of making a good confession.

2. Instead of the catechism, the mistress will have the boarders consider the Ten Commandments, the commandments of the Church, and the seven mortal sins[29] as they examine their conscience. As references, she may use the *Conduct* of Saint François de Sales,[30] the works of the Archbishop of Paris, Grenade's method,[31] or other writings that will help the boarders understand the sacrament. She may also compose her own lesson.

3. She will then have the boarders compose acts of contrition following the examples proposed by Louis de Grenade, such as the one in the *Paradise of Prayer*[32] that begins: "Who will give water for my head?" or an act of contrition from Book 2 of Father Saint Jure's *Knowledge and Love of Our Savior*,[33] or some other act of contrition.

4. At a convenient time, she will meet separately with each girl to instruct her individually. She should follow the recommendations given in chapter four, section II. She can then send the boarders one at a time into the church or to some other place of devotion where they can prepare themselves and make their acts of contrition.

5. On the day after all the boarders have confessed, the mistresses will ask them to continue making acts of contrition that acknowledge their sorrow for their sins and their firm intention to mend their ways and that cause them to consider how Our Lord has pardoned their sins but also has given them the obligation to avoid sin and to keep their souls clean and pure if they wish to be worthy temples of God.

---

29. These are also known as the seven deadly sins, first enumerated by Pope Gregory I in the sixth century: pride, covetousness, lust, envy, gluttony, anger, and sloth (*Encyclopedia Britannica*, accessed April 15, 2020, https://www.britannica.com/topic/seven-deadly-sins).

30. a Véritable conduite de Saint François de Sales pour la confession et la communion, fidèlement *extraite de ses écrits*, ed. Adrien Gambart (Paris: Hérissant, 1748).

31. Luis de Grenada (1504–88), Spanish Dominican preacher and devotional writer. This is probably a reference to Granada's two-volume *Sinner's Guide* (1556–57).

32. *Le Paradis des prières* (Paris: Chez Eustache Foucauld, 1603).

33. Jean-Baptiste Saint-Jure (1588–1657), Jesuit priest, educator and devotional writer, author of *De la connaissance et de l'amour du fils de Dieu* (On the Knowledge and Love of God) (1634).

v.

Final Preparation

1. In the final week, the mistress will meet privately with every girl, teaching each one individually about the intentions she should have and the dispositions she should bring to the sacrament. She will speak to them about the Holy Sacrifice of the Mass, telling them how they should try to hear mass on the day of their First Communion and how to make a prayer of thanksgiving.

2. She will quicken their desire to practice virtue and good works, all the more so because the time of their happiness is near.

3. Two days before their First Communion, these boarders will be taken out of their normal classroom and taught in a separate area. They will only be in the company of the other boarders during church services, meals, and in the dormitories at night. For these two days, they will attend vespers and matins, and the mistress will have them perform other devotions, such as visiting the chapels and oratories of the convent, where they can pray to their patron saints for the grace to be worthy of receiving the sacrament.

4. The day before their First Communion, the mistress will accompany these girls to the Mother Superior's rooms. They will thank the Mother Superior for the excellent preparation she has arranged for them to receive. They will ask for her blessing and implore her to request that all of the nuns ask God to bless them.

5. They will then go to the General Mistress's rooms, asking her forgiveness for anything they might have done to displease her, thanking her for the good preparation they received from her, and requesting her prayers on their behalf. They will do the same with their Class Mistresses.

6. They will also ask their fellow boarders, not only those in their classes but all the others, to pardon their faults.

7. That same day, the mistress will lead the communicants into the church and up to the altar rail to show them how to receive communion. She will instruct them to curtsy, both before and after they receive the host, to keep their hands clasped and their eyes lowered. When the priest comes to them, they cover their hands and open their mouths properly, sticking out their tongues to the edge of their lips.

8. She will also remind them of the state of mind they should have as they hear mass, and she will give each girl her own copy of the mass so that those girls who cannot say the prayers by themselves have something to do and a useful source of help.

9. Thirty minutes before mass on the day of their First Communion, the mistress will remind them briefly of the intentions they should have and will explain some point of Christ's Passion on which they can meditate during mass.

10. The new communicants will remain separated from the other boarders the rest of that day, and if possible, they will attend a mass of thanksgiving the following day. Afterward, either the General Mistress or the Class Mistress who has prepared the girls for communion will take them back to their classroom and exhort them to profit from the grace they have just received by demonstrating through all of their actions how highly they esteem the sacrament.

11. Before these boarders receive communion again, the mistress will review her previous instructions, especially those concerning the Holy Sacrament of the Altar. She will repeat the intentions and preparation the boarders should have made before they approach the altar rail as well as their state of mind as they hear mass. The mistress should devote an hour of catechism class each day for a week to this review.

CHAPTER SIX

The Writing Mistress

1. The Writing Mistress must devote herself to teaching the boarders to write. She will arrive at every class punctually and spend all the allotted time at this task.

2. The first thing she must teach the boarders is how to hold the feather pen correctly with three fingers. Afterward, she will teach them to form the letters *o* and *i*, whose strokes are the foundation of all the other letters, followed by *a, u, m, n*. However, she should not move on to these four letters until the boarders have mastered the first two. Then she will give them the letters with upstrokes and downstrokes, *b, d, 1, f, g, h,* starting first with the easiest ones to form.[34]

3. Once the boarders are capable of forming all the letters, she will give

---

34. The French term used in the text is *lettres passantes*. Richelet, the author of the first French dictionary (Geneva, 1680), defines *passant* as "participe qui signifie qui surpasse, qui surmonte" (present participle meaning that which goes beyond or above). A "lettre passante" was one that had a pen stroke higher or lower than the base strokes of the letter.

them *liaisons*[35] like *uuu, mmm, nnn,* then words that do not contain letters with upstrokes or downstrokes, like the following: *avancement, commune, communauté, commis.* She will have them write three rows of each word to strengthen the hand. Next she will give them longer words containing letters with upstrokes or downstrokes, like *honorablement, supplications, compagnies.* When the boarders have mastered these words adequately, she will give them a whole line of words, then two lines. She will also show them how to form the two systems of numerals, that is, the Roman and the Arabic.[36]

4. From the beginning, she will teach them to leave an equal space between the strokes that form the letters and to leave only the space of one letter between each word.

5. Experience has shown that this is the most useful method for teaching writing. Nevertheless, the mistress is not obligated to follow this method exactly if she judges it appropriate to change some part of it.

6. She will spend the entire class time working with the boarders individually. She will first write a few words for all to imitate and then correct mistakes, showing each girl the proper dimensions of each letter. She will work with the least capable girls first, because they need her help more than the others. She will guide their hands with hers to give them more confidence in their handwriting. Such guidance is especially recommended when teaching beginners and should be used every day for about six weeks.

7. Until the boarders have mastered handwriting, she must not allow them to write on anything but the paper she has given them, because to do so will spoil their handwriting. She must teach them to write neatly, without smearing ink on their paper or on their clothes. For this purpose, she will always put a few little pieces of canvas or old taffeta on each table that can be used to wipe pens.[37]

8. She will make sure that the boarders spend the entire class time working. They may only speak to ask necessary questions and must do so in a low

35. The word *liaison,* as it is used here, is a technical term in orthography. Richelet defines it as "Terme de Maître à écrire. Petit trait de plume qui lie les parties des lettres les unes aux autres" (Writing Teacher's term, pen stroke that unites the parts of letters one to another). The letters *u, m,* and *n,* all without downstrokes or upstrokes, are formed by *liaison,* that is, the final pen stroke of the first letter moves into the first stroke of the second letter, and so on.

36. The text refers to Arabic numerals as "sauvage," that is, "savage" or "barbarous." *Barbarous* signifies that which does not have Latin (that is, Roman) roots.

37. Both canvas and taffeta made from silk are tightly woven fabrics that are somewhat water resistant. Ink would not have soaked through these fabrics onto the worktable or the girls' hands.

voice. The mistress will observe the same rule and not speak to the boarders about anything unrelated to handwriting. She must make sure, above all, that the boarders have good posture and sit up straight as they write. She must not allow those who slump to write as much as the other boarders.

9. If a boarder asks for permission to write to her parents, the mistress will help her with the letter and insist on correct handwriting and spelling.

10. With the agreement of the General Mistress, she will teach those boarders who are fairly adept at writing to sharpen pens.

11. When a group of boarders has mastered handwriting, the Writing Mistress will let the Class Mistress know that they are ready to study spelling.

12. If any boarders won't do their writing assignments, or if they make noise and cause disorder that prevents the other boarders from writing, the Writing Mistress will call their attention to their behavior and correct them. If they continue to misbehave, she will report them either to the General Mistress or to their Class Mistresses.

13. After each writing assignment is finished, the Writing Mistress will collect any papers that require examples of good handwriting to imitate. These examples will take the form of maxims or pious verses of one or two lines that the mistress has prepared previously outside of class and that will not take too much time to copy. She will include these examples with the collected papers and then take them back after the lesson for further use. She herself may also write on the papers from time to time.

14. She will take great care of all the materials for which she is responsible: pens, paper, and inkwells. She will keep everything clean and make sure that the ink does not become too thick. She will add new ink from time to time, as well as cotton when it is needed. She will lock up everything in a cabinet found in the room where the boarders write. She will keep the key to the cabinet.

15. On all of the papers, she will write the boarders' first and last names. She will keep all papers in her cabinet, separating them according to class.

16. She will ask the Bursar to provide everything she requires to teach writing. She will furnish the boarders with paper and ink as well as the pens needed in spelling lessons and any materials used in arithmetic.

17. If the school does not have printed circulars of feast days to distribute, the Writing Mistress will select, at the end of each month, those boarders with the best handwriting and have them compose circulars announcing the patron saints of each class, noting the saint's name, feast day, a virtue associated with the saint, and a prayer for the saint's patronage in a special need.

18. If there are large numbers of boarders in every class, the Writing Mistress will have another teacher to help her. This second teacher will observe all of the rules given in the previous paragraphs of this chapter, will compose some of the examples of good handwriting herself, and will help the Writing Mistress show the boarders how to write.

19. If there are three writing classes, the second teacher must be present at two of them at least. The Writing Mistress must do the same.

CHAPTER SEVEN
The Needlework Mistress

1. The Needlework Mistress will always arrive punctually at the hour designated for her class (if the class begins exactly at 8:15 in the morning and then again right after recess, the mistress can wait fifteen minutes before arriving at the later class). She will devote herself entirely to instruction in her subject and never allow anything to distract her from this duty.

2. She will teach the girls patiently and assiduously, always encouraging them to do their best. She will examine their work frequently and, if necessary, demonstrate how to sew correctly. If the girls have made mistakes, she will make them undo the mistakes and redo the work correctly. She will teach them to knot their threads, whether of wool or silk, and to handle cloth. If at all possible, she will have a daily assistant who works with the girls in groups of two or three at a time. This will enable the Needlework Mistress to spend more time in instruction.

3. She will begin the boarders' training with the easiest and most important types of sewing, such as making a straight seam and a hem; or the cross-stitch on a piece of simple canvas or on cloth; and then tapestry with counted stitches and painter's stitch.[38] Afterward, the mistress can show them other forms of needlework, such as how to embroider flowers, how to embroider with gold or silver thread, how to make both French- and English-style lace, and any other types of needlework commonly done in the school's region or that the parents of the boarders wish their daughters to learn.

38. The "point compté" (counted stitch) requires the embroiderer to count the number of threads on the cloth for each stitch. The "point de peintre" (painter's stitch) uses many different lengths of stitches to create artistic designs.

4. She will take care to keep the needlework, woolen cloth, silk, etc., stored in a cabinet or chest designated for that purpose, or she will give the responsibility to a boarder who has been appointed by the Class Mistress. She will teach this boarder how to arrange everything in a clean and orderly manner. She will also see that nothing is wasted and that the material is properly cared for. When the Linen Mistress informs her that a boarder's personal linen needs mending, she will show the boarder how to do this correctly.[39] At times, she can also teach boarders to mend their dresses.

5. When she needs woolen cloth, silk, needles, etc., she will make a list and give it to the Class Mistress.

6. She will not waste time conversing with the boarders about useless subjects and will pay no heed to the girls' complaints or grumblings about their Class Mistresses. Rather, she will make every effort to have the girls hold their mistresses in high esteem and to treat them with the respect and obedience that is the mistress's due.

7. Nor will she talk to the borders about their classmates' shortcomings but only to the Class Mistress.

CHAPTER EIGHT

The Mistress Who Teaches Arithmetic,
Reading, Handwriting, and Spelling

1. She will arrive in class on time to teach the boarders to read, count, and do sums.

2. She will teach arithmetic in the following way: first, she will teach them the nine Arabic numerals as well as their corresponding Roman numerals; then she will have them count to 1,000, then do simple sums by arranging jetons[40] correctly; then she will have them go over their answers while she checks for mistakes; then she will have them perform more difficult calculations to the extent of their abilities.

3. She will also teach them other types of arithmetic, for example: how much is 7×7, 5×5, and such, beginning with the easiest numbers. To improve

---

39. Here *linge* (linen) refers to undergarments.

40. A "jeton" was a token or medal in the shape of a coin that could be used for counting or calculation.

their facility with arithmetic, she will have them calculate how much they spend on purchases. For example, if they buy 15 *aunes*[41] of gold braid[42] at the cost of 5 *sols* 4 *deniers*[43] per *aune*, what is the total cost? She should first have them count to determine the cost and then pay in several denominations of coins. She will also teach them to write numbers and, with the more capable girls, how to do simple arithmetic with pen and paper.

4. She will only work with one or two boarders at a time to help them understand better. She will use all class time teaching, without talking about any other subject or allowing the girls to engage in any other occupation. She should observe this rule in everything else that she teaches.

5. She will have ready a sheet of paper with examples of many types of numbers and word problems that she can use for teaching arithmetic and counting in the method described above.

6. When it is time to move from arithmetic to reading manuscript, she will have the boarders read while seated in rows. If the boarders are numerous, she will have some of them read one day and others the next.

7. When working with beginning boarders, she will start with the easiest readings, making certain that the girls recognize the letters of the alphabet and any abbreviations. She will ask them to read aloud, a few at a time, encouraging them, as much as possible, to identify words on their own.

8. For spelling, she will first obtain as many copies of the same book, in print, as there are boarders who will read on any day. She may need as many as eight or ten books.

9. She will give each girl a clean sheet of paper. She will then dictate, word for word, two or three lines from the above-mentioned books, which the boarders will write on their papers. Afterward, she will give each girl one of the books so that the girl can correct any mistakes herself. The girl will do this by writing the correct form of the word above any word she has misspelled. Then the mistress will have the girls write out the same three lines a second time without looking at what they had written previously. The next day, the girls will write out the same lines yet again, taking care to write clearly, on a clean sheet of paper. They will continue rewriting these lines until they make no more mistakes.

41. Approximately four feet.
42. To trim or edge clothing or linen.
43. The *sol*, or *sou*, equaled one-twentieth of a pound, *livre*, of silver. The *denier* was one-twelfth of a *sol*.

10. There is another method the mistress may use if she prefers. She will give each boarder a notebook. She will read from a book three or four lines, which the class will write. Then she will have one boarder spell aloud each word, letter by letter, of the text, and the other boarders will make corrections. The mistress will check their corrections for accuracy. The next day, the mistress will have the class write the same lines on a new sheet of paper to reinforce the lesson.

11. The Bursar will furnish the books for spelling and the jetons for counting. For any other needs, the mistress should address the Writing Mistress.

12. She will not speak of any boarder's deficiencies to anyone besides the Class Mistress.

CHAPTER NINE

The Bursar

1. The duties of the Bursar are: to safeguard the money of those boarders who are not able to do so themselves; to keep a record of all clothing and furnishings boarders bring into the convent and to take responsibility for these things; to provide the boarders with anything they need, if that is the parents' wish.

2. As soon as a girl enters the convent as a boarder, the Bursar will make a list of the girl's clothes, silverware, tableware, etc.

3. The Bursar will keep two books. In the first, she will note the name of each boarder as well as the day, month, and year she entered the school and then the list of what the boarder brought with her. In the second book, the Bursar will write whatever goods she provides the boarder. When she is paid for the goods she has provided, she will cancel these charges.

4. When a boarder's parents ask for the child's old clothing, the Bursar will erase from the first book anything she has returned to the parents. She will do the same with any clothing the parents desire to be given to the poor, and she will give such clothing to the General Mistress.

5. Whenever she learns that a boarder is withdrawing from school, she will quickly notify the Linen Mistress so that together they can account for all of the boarder's personal linen. If the Bursar finds something missing, she will make a note and return the missing items without delay.

6. From time to time, she will supply the boarders with shoes, gloves,

combs, ribbons, silks in a variety of colors, different sorts of thread, sewing needles and thimbles, pins, shoe laces, *équillettes*,[44] and other such personal needs.

7. She will also have reams of paper, pieces of cardboard to put over the paper as protection, penknives, pens, and ink to supply to the Writing Mistress. She will only buy quantities of these things proportional to the number of boarders so that she does not have to get rid of any excessive supplies.

8. The Treasurer will give the Bursar, in advance, the amount of money needed to buy supplies.[45] When she leaves her position of authority, or more frequently if the Mother Superior deems it appropriate, the Bursar will give an accounting of this money, preferably in the presence of the General Mistress and an assistant.

9. She will determine the boarders' needs after consulting the lists of these needs drawn up by the Class Mistresses. Every three months, she will give the Linen Mistress supplies to mend the boarders' linen, such as heavy thread for sheets and other types of thread for personal linen. She will also supply those nuns who care for the community's clothing with as much thread and cloth as they require.

10. She will designate a day and time for the boarders of each class to come to her office (with the permission of the Class Mistress) and receive the supplies listed by the mistress. She will only work with two or three boarders at a time and take care not to delay them from returning to class quickly.

11. She will not buy anything else, whether for needlework or other class needs, or if requested by an individual boarder, without the General Mistress's permission.

12. She will give the nuns at the convent gate a list of what they should buy for the boarders on the days when they are free to do so. She will make an inventory of what they have bought and note all purchases in her book.

13. When there are enough shoes that require repair, she will give them to the cobbler, keeping the shoes of each boarder together and separate from the others. The cobbler will return the shoes to the Bursar in the same fashion once he has repaired them. The Bursar will also mend the boarders' clothing and stockings when necessary, but she will never remake any clothing. For example, she will not change an outer garment like a skirt into an inner garment without the General Mistress's permission.

44. Simple piece of jewelry to decorate a blouse or jacket.
45. I have translated the term *dépositaire*, literally, the "custodian," as "treasurer."

14. When a boarder enters the school, the Bursar will find out from the General Mistress if the parents want the school to provide all of the girl's needs, and she will write this information in her book.

15. She will prepare an invoice to give to the parents when they bring the money for their child's room and board. She will receive the money from the parents.

16. On each boarder's invoice, she will note the charge of two or three *sous* per quarter for pens, ink, thread, and cloth. She will charge less for those boarders who arrive with new clothing and linen that require less mending. For those boarders whose parents do not expect the school to supply any personal needs, the Bursar will have the General Mistress ask the parents to contribute some money for the general needs of all the boarders.

17. The Bursar may not make any profit from these supplies. She must charge the boarders the same amount that she pays for goods, even if she has them at a cheaper price than that normally charged in the city. The only money she may charge beyond the cost is for the transport of goods, the reimbursement of any damages that may have occurred, and for the general supplies of penknives and paper for letters and spelling class.

18. When she gives an accounting of her receipts and expenses to the Mother Superior and finds, as she examines the transactions in detail, that she has more money than she needs but that this money cannot be equitably divided among the individual boarders, she will see that this money is used for class oratories or for needlework supplies or for little prizes that the boarders merit.

19. She is also charged with the duty of accompanying the General Mistress to the parlor when the latter speaks to the boarders' parents unless the Mother Superior has assigned someone else to this task. She will also accompany the boarders to the parlor in the absence of the General Mistress.

CHAPTER TEN
The Linen Mistress

1. The Linen Mistress will take good care of the boarders' linen. She will clean it, bleach it, and preserve it from damage.

2. When a girl enters the boarding school, the Linen Mistress will receive her linen, count it, and write the quantity in her book. She will return this same linen to the girl when she leaves the school, after examining the iden-

tification mark on each piece to make sure that the linen does not belong to another boarder.

3. She will ensure that not only the personal linen but also the dresses, stockings, and shoes of each boarder have identification marks. She will note each identification mark at the end of her list of the boarder's linen.

4. In the same book, she will note any new linen the boarder has received while in the school. She will exchange the old linen for this new linen and give the old linen to the General Mistress or the Bursar.

5. She will keep the keys to the linen chests of those boarders who are not capable of caring for their own linen. She will give them clean linen twice a week, or more often if the General Mistress deems it necessary. She will bring the clean linen to their beds on Wednesday and Saturday. In winter, she will dry the linen before distributing it.

6. Every six months or so, she will examine the linen chests of the boarders who care for their own linen to see if any linen has been damaged. She will teach the boarders how to care for their linen, how to make use of each piece, and how to store the linen properly.

7. She will make separate bundles of each boarder's laundry so that nothing is lost in the wash. She will show the older boarders how to make their own bundles.

8. Every week, she will give all the boarders' linens to the Linen Mistress of the convent to be included with the nuns' linen, whether it is sent out of the convent for washing or cleaned in the convent. When she receives the clean linen, she will count it and have it brought to her room. Then each class of boarders will come to her room, one after the other, and fold the linen. The Linen Mistress will teach them to fold correctly. She may also bring the clean linen to each classroom for folding if the General Mistress approves.

9. Every week, she will scrub the boarders' collars and neckerchiefs with soap and water. She will hang them to dry on a fir plank or on a small table, or she can dry them with small irons or some other way that is practiced in her region.

10. She will mend the linen of the boarders who cannot do so by themselves. For that of the older boarders, she will make a list of what requires mending and give the list and the linen to the Needlework Mistress to teach the boarders how to mend.

11. In addition to the boarders' linen, she is responsible for their stockings and repaired shoes. She will go to the dormitories once or twice a week to examine these shoes and stockings, removing any that need mending and

replacing them with others. She can carry out this task more easily if each dormitory is equipped with an armoire or chest containing serviceable shoes and stockings. Whenever a boarder requires new shoes or stockings, the Linen Mistress should send her to the Bursar.

12. Every week or two, she will bring the Bursar all the shoes and stockings that require repair. First, she will place the boarder's identification mark on all clothing and make a list of what belongs to each girl. She will give this list to the Bursar, who, in turn, will enter everything in her book. When the repairs have been made, the Bursar will return everything to the Linen Mistress.

13. When a boarder requires new personal linen, the Linen Mistress will make a list of these needs and give it to the General Mistress, who will ask the boarder's parents to send it to the school.

14. The Bursar will provide the Linen Mistress with supplies for the general use of the boarders, such as heavy thread to mend bed linens and other types of thread to mend personal linen. If ever the Linen Mistress of the convent has too much work and the Bursar very little, the Bursar may assume responsibility for shoes and stockings, leaving the Linen Mistress with only the linen to care for. If the Bursar has too much work, however, it is the Mother Superior of the convent who will relieve her of the care of the boarders' personal linen described in the preceding paragraph.

CHAPTER ELEVEN

The Sisters[46] *Who Dress and Groom the Boarders*

1. The nuns appointed to dress and groom the boarders will arrive punctually in the dormitories at the hour of rising to care for the boarders assigned to them by the mistresses. Normally, they will care for the same boarders every day.

2. They will comb each boarder's hair back in order to rub the head with a brush or a cap of rough cloth, making sure that the scalp and hair are very clean.

---

46. The term *sister* refers to a converse nun. Converse nuns were women of low social rank who were not allowed to teach or be in a position of authority. They took simple vows of poverty, chastity, and obedience but not the fourth vow, to teach, taken by Ursuline choir nuns. They performed the domestic tasks of the convent, such as cooking, cleaning, and running errands. In an Ursuline convent, where the choir nuns were not allowed to leave the convent, the converse nuns served as a connection between the convent and the outside world.

They will not be hasty but take all the time necessary for grooming. In the winter, they will repeat this grooming once or twice a day to ensure cleanliness.

3. They will arrange the hair of those boarders who cannot do so themselves simply and practically.

4. To prevent the boarders from catching cold in the winter, they will bring shoes and stockings to their beds and make certain they are sufficiently dressed before being groomed so they do not have bare heads for very long.

5. The nuns who dress the youngest boarders will wake them and put on their shoes while they are still in bed, or these nuns can let the girls put their shoes on by themselves if they are able to do so. Then they will do nothing more until the little boarders have said their morning prayers, pronouncing them well. Afterward, they will perform the grooming, arrange the girls' hair, dress them, and put away the girls' combs and brushes in their nightstands, or they may show the girls how to put these things away properly.

CHAPTER TWELVE
The Sisters in Charge of the Dormitories

1. There will be a Converse Sister in each dormitory to make the beds, care for the boarders' clothing, etc.

2. These sisters will treat the boarders respectfully and with kindness, never taking it upon themselves to reprimand or punish their charges. If, however, the boarder does something offensive, the sister can point out this behavior gently if the mistress is not present, or afterward she can report this behavior to the mistress, who will reprimand the boarder. The sister will not stop her work to talk to boarders about unnecessary things.

3. Following morning prayers, the Converse Sisters will go to the dormitories to awaken the boarders, groom those assigned to them, and light a fire in the winter.

4. While the boarders are dressing, the sister will make the beds correctly, and after mass, they will clean and tidy up the dormitories.

5. After evening prayer, they will put out the boarders' nightclothes. In winter, they will close the windows if they are open and prepare the chimney stove so that it is ready to light when the boarders enter the dormitory to undress.

6. They will also bring water so the boarders can wash their hands. The best way to ensure that water is available is to have in each dormitory, if at all possi-

ble, a little water container made of tin or copper that opens with a spigot, with a bowl underneath and a hand towel that is changed two or three times a week.

7. They will clean the boarders' dresses and stockings as often as necessary to keep the clothing neat and clean. If a boarder has a change of clothing, the sister will put it in an armoire or chest after having cleaned it well and folded it properly.

8. They will mend any clothing that has been ripped or torn. If the mending requires more than an hour, the sister will give the clothing to the Bursar, who will arrange for the mending.

9. They will return any clothing the boarders have outgrown to the General Mistress or to the Bursar. They will not dispose of outgrown or worn-out clothing in any other way.

10. When a boarder leaves the convent, the sister will pack up all of the girl's belongings and give them to the Bursar.

11. She will clean the combs and brushes of the boarders every day, except for those of the oldest boarders, which she will clean three or four times a week.

12. She will carry the boarders' dirty linen to the appointed place.

13. In the winter, she will bring firewood to the dormitories and classrooms.

14. Whenever a boarder has permission to remain in bed later in the morning, the sister will wake her up at the time designated by the Class Mistress, dress her, and groom her. If the boarder stays in bed because she is ill, the sister will bring her everything she needs and ask for instructions from the General Mistress or the Nurse as to how she should care for the ill boarder until the boarder is admitted to the infirmary.

15. The sister will mend the bed curtains, blankets, and mattresses of both horsehair and straw. She will not take apart any mattresses belonging to the boarders either to make them shorter or to enlarge them without the permission of the Treasurer or the General Mistress.

16. Every week, she will ask the Linen Mistress for clean hand towels, and she will bring back the dirty ones. She will do the same with the cloths she uses to clean the furniture.

17. She will learn by memory to identify all of the objects used for dressing and grooming that belong to the dormitory so that nothing is misplaced. Every dormitory will have an armoire, where these objects are kept. The sister will have the key to the armoire.

18. Every month, she will scrub clean the bowls, chamber pots, and anything else for which she is responsible.

19. When the bed curtains and blankets require cleaning and it is time to take the mattresses apart to clean them, she will notify the Assistant Mother of the Converse Nuns so this assistant can send another sister to help with the work. The sister in charge of a class's dormitory will mark every piece of the bedding she has taken apart so she can put everything back together more easily.

20. Normally, the sisters will sleep in the boarders' dormitories unless the Mother Superior tells them to do otherwise. They will arrive in the dormitories at 8:15 in the evening and remain there until the end of morning prayers. They will not allow the boarders to engage in conversation while in bed or to get up during the night or to engage in other disorderly behavior. If a boarder falls sick, they will come to her aid and inform the General Mistress of the boarder's condition, if necessary. When a sister gets out of bed to help a boarder, she will wear at least her short veil. If any sister has been obliged to stay awake for a long period during the night, she can stay in bed until 5:30 a.m.[47]

21. There will be a lit lamp in every dormitory or, at least, a chimney fire near the dormitory to provide light in case any problem arises during the night.

CHAPTER THIRTEEN
Schedule the Boarders Will Observe

I.

1. There is no specific uniform for boarders. They will dress as their parents wish, always observing the customs of modesty and decorum. They may not wear anything vain or superfluous, and the bosom must be covered.

2. Their hair will be arranged in a modest way befitting their social condition, without being curled or powdered.

3. When assembling, they will always remain in the place that the General Mistress has assigned them. This place corresponds to the boarder's age and ability.

4. Their living quarters will be separate from those of the nuns. They will not enter any parts of the premises reserved for the nuns, such as the dormitories, chapter rooms, refectory, common room, or novitiate, without the express permission of the Mother Superior.

---

47. This paragraph tells us that the normal time for waking was earlier than 5:30 a.m.

5. They may leave the convent to see their fathers and mothers, or guardians, but they may not spend the night outside of the convent, except in the following circumstances: a parent or guardian falls gravely ill or dies; parents or guardians have traveled a long way to make a rare visit; the boarder is asked to serve as sponsor at a baptism; attendance at the vesture[48] or profession of a sister or other close relative that takes place in a different city; any other situation that the Mother Superior deems so important that she cannot refuse permission.

6. Because the boarders are divided into classes, as stated in chapter one, each class will have a patron saint to whom they dedicate the class oratory. There may also be another patron saint for the whole school.

II.
Daily Schedule

1. The boarders will rise at 5:30 or 6:00 a.m., whichever time the Mother Superior judges appropriate. During the coldest winter months, they are not obliged to awaken before 6:30, or even later, if there is no mass before 8:00.

2. They will be dressed when they go to their oratory or classroom to say their prescribed prayers by 6:45 a.m. In the winter, they can say their prayers in their bedrooms in front of a pious painting if the oratory is too far away.

3. They will then go to mass, which is said at 7:00 a.m. After mass, they will have breakfast, and thirty minutes later, they will go to their classrooms to begin their reading lesson, needlework, etc.

4. At 10:00 a.m., the lessons end and the boarders will put away their books and needlework. At 10:15, they will say the Litanies of the Virgin.

5. Immediately afterward, they will go to the dining hall. During the midday meal, one of the boarders will read while standing at a slightly elevated lectern in the middle of the room. She will read the text the mistress has chosen twice. Then she will take her place at table and dine.

6. When they have finished eating and said their grace after the meal, the boarders will go to recess until 12:15 p.m., at which time they will return to their classrooms and work on the same lessons as in the morning.

7. On days of fast and abstinence, they will finish their morning lessons

---

48. The ceremony during which a postulant to a religious order receives the habit she will wear during her years in the novitiate.

half an hour later because their midday meal, as well as that of the nuns, is served half an hour later. Recess will follow the meal.

8. At about 2:00 p.m., they will stop their classwork and put away their books and needlework, just as they did in the morning. The older boarders will say vespers and the little ones some other prayer. They will then have their afternoon snack.

9. At 3:00 p.m., after the classroom has been tidied up, they will spend a good quarter of an hour studying catechism in pairs. Or, if they do not know their prayers, they can study them. Afterward, the mistress will teach spelling to those boarders who are advanced enough to learn, and the others can work on another subject. They will stop all work at 4:00 p.m.

10. Catechism class will begin at 4:15 p.m. On the days when there is no catechism lesson, the boarders should spend at least fifteen minutes reading either a text assigned to the entire class or of each girl's choosing; pray together or engage in some other devotion; or do needlework. On Saturdays, instead of catechism class, boarders will attend the Exposition or Benediction of the Blessed Sacrament or engage in a devotional exercise in honor of the patron saint of their class.

11. At 5:00 p.m., they will go to the dining hall for supper, during which they will listen to another reading, but the reading will not be repeated a second time.

12. After saying grace, they will have recess. In the winter, recess ends at 6:45 p.m., at least for the youngest boarders, and at 7:00 p.m. in the summer. The older boarders will go to their oratory and say privately the matins and lauds[49] of the Little Office of the Virgin Mary (at times, the boarders should be permitted to say the office aloud, in two parts).[50] Then these boarders will examine their conscience in the manner described in their prayer book. They will get undressed and be in bed by 8:00 p.m. In the winter, they may say their evening prayers in their bedrooms if the oratory is too cold. They may also have recess in their bedrooms in the winter so they can begin to get ready for bed more comfortably.

49. Lauds, or matins, designates the first psalms and prayers of the Divine Office said at daybreak. According to the *Catholic Encyclopedia*, in spite of its title, matins were said at night at the end of vigils or simply as evening prayer (vol. M, accessed June 9, 2020, https://www.newadvent.org/cathen/10050a.htm).

50. Le Petit Office de la Vierge Marie (Little Office of Our Lady) is a shorter version of the Divine Office containing such prayers as the Magnificat, which was used commonly in the seventeenth century by non-contemplative religious orders of both women and men (*Catholic Encyclopedia*, vol. L, accessed June 9, 2020, newadvent.org/cathen/09294.htm).

13. The young boarders will examine their conscience, say their prayers, and be in bed at 7:45 p.m.

14. Each class will have its own designated time, both in the morning and afternoon, to work in the writing classroom. If there are three classes that must use this space, one will have the lesson in the morning, from 8:15 until 9:15 a.m., and the two others from 12:15 until 2:15 p.m.

15. On days of fast and abstinence, two of the classes, or even all three if it is more convenient, will use the writing room in the morning.

III.

Sundays and Feast Days

1. In the convents where there is no low mass before the high mass said at 8:00 a.m., the boarders can sleep until 6:30. In the convents where there is a low mass, the boarders will awaken at the usual time to hear the low mass as well as a part of the high mass, according to what the Mother Superior deems appropriate.

2. The older boarders will attend vespers and complins,[51] the younger ones only vespers. If there is a sermon after vespers, all boarders will listen to it and then eat their snack during complins, whether complins take place before or after the sermon.

3. If there is no sermon, the boarders will occupy themselves for about thirty minutes after recess with some pious reading, either privately or as a group, or else they will perform some devotional exercise assigned by the Class Mistress. The younger boarders are excused from this exercise.

4. On feast days, when the entire Divine Office is said, the boarders will attend from the first vespers to complins as well as matins. The older boarders will stay until the homily begins, but the other boarders will leave earlier, according to the order established by the Mother Superior.

5. On the days when they are to receive communion, the boarders will spend fifteen minutes in prayer before mass. If there is a low mass before high mass, the boarders will receive communion at the low mass and hear the high mass afterward. If there is only one mass, they will say prayers of thanksgiving for half an hour after this mass. On those days the boarders will also pray for fifteen minutes before supper.

51. Complins is the final part of the Divine Office said in the evening.

CHAPTER FOURTEEN
Schedule for Extraordinary Days

I.

1. On Christmas Eve, the boarders will have supper at 4:30 p.m.; they will examine their conscience at 5:45 and go to bed immediately after this.

2. The Converse Sisters assigned to each class will awaken the boarders at 11:00 at night so they can be ready to go to church before the midnight mass begins. When mass is over, the boarders will return to their rooms and go back to sleep. If any boarders have received communion, they will remain in church another fifteen minutes to say prayers of thanksgiving. The youngest boarders will not go to midnight mass. They will sleep until it is time for the mass held at daybreak. The other boarders will be out of bed by 7:30 and hear a low mass, if possible. Then all the boarders will have breakfast together before high mass, which everyone attends. The Converse Sisters will remain with the boarders in their care from Christmas Eve until they accompany the boarders to mass on Christmas Day.

3. A few days before the Feast of the Purification of the Blessed Virgin Mary,[52] the Class Mistresses must remember to ask the boarders to request candles of their parents or of the Bursar. The night before the feast day, each class will make its own bundle of candles and give the bundle to the Sacristan,[53] who will see that the boarders' candles, along with those of the nuns, are given to a priest for blessing.

4. During the distribution of the candles that have been blessed, the mistresses will give each boarder a candle. Once the candles have been lit, the girls will form a procession in two rows, with the oldest girls in a class at the front and the mistress at the tail end of her class. All processions will observe this same order.

5. On Ash Wednesday, if there aren't many boarders, they may receive ashes at the main altar rail used by the nuns. If there are many boarders and two priests are available, the boarders will receive ashes at the side altar rail.

---

52. February 2.

53. The Sacristan (the feminine form in French is *Sacristine*) had charge of the sacristy, that is, the part of the church where the priest's vestments, chalices, and such were kept. One of her duties was to obtain objects used in special ceremonies, such as the candles for Candlemas and palms for Palm Sunday, for both the school and the cloister.

The boarders should have their heads uncovered enough so that the priest can place the ashes on their forehead. They should take off their gloves and take their place in line, according to their rank in class, and curtsy before and after receiving ashes.

6. From the first Saturday of Lent until Holy Thursday, the boarders' reading and needlework lessons will end at 10:45.

7. At 11:00, the boarders will go to vespers and then say the litanies.

8. They will have their midday meal at 11:15 and a snack at 2:30.

9. Catechism will take place at 4:30, but before the lesson begins, the boarders will say complins. They will have supper at 5:15.

10. All other activities will take place according to the schedule for ordinary days.

11. On the eves and days when the complete Divine Office is said, they will attend complins.

12. On Palm Sunday, after the benediction, the Sacristan will give the mistresses the palms to distribute to the boarders, following the directions given previously for the distribution of candles. The boarders will stand up holding their palms and take part in the procession. After this, the boarders will have breakfast if they have already been to the low mass. They will then return to church to hear the reading of the Passion and stay for the end of the high mass. If there is only one mass, the boarders will have breakfast before the procession.

13. The three final days of Holy Week, the boarders will take part in the *Tenebrae*.[54] The oldest will remain for lauds; the youngest will follow the same schedule as on the days when they attend matins. The boarders will have supper at 5:30 p.m., examine their conscience, and go to bed at the usual time.

14. On Holy Thursday, after the boarders have gotten dressed, they will go to church to say their prayers, or they can engage in reflection on the sacred mysteries celebrated during these days if that is what the mistress has assigned to them. They will spend about half an hour in church and then have

54. *Tenebrae*, Latin for "darkness," or the Mass and Office of Darkness, is an ancient custom celebrated on the Wednesday, Thursday, and Friday of Holy Week. It is called "Tenebrae" because the services begin in the late afternoon and end in the evening, when night has fallen. The ceremony includes the singing of matins and lauds as well as the Lamentations of Jeremiah and involves the lighting and gradual extinguishing of candles to signify Christ's Crucifixion on Good Friday (see "Holy Week," *Catholic Encyclopedia*, vol. H, accessed June 8, 2020, https://www.newadvent.org/cathen/07435a.htm).

breakfast. Afterward, the mistress who is *en semaine* will have them read, do needlework, or something else useful. The boarders will not have writing class from Holy Thursday until after Easter Monday.

15. The boarders will attend high mass and vespers before taking their midday meal.

16. When the signal for the *Mandatum*[55] has been given, the boarders will enter the church for the ceremony.

17. On Good Friday, the boarders will dress and go to the monstrance altar[56] to pray for fifteen minutes. When the signal for the sermon is given, they will go into church to hear it. When the sermon has ended, they will leave church for a short time. The younger boarders and anyone else who needs to eat something will be given a little bread. Then all will return to church for the end of the service.

18. During the time when the nuns are engaged in Adoration of the Cross, the boarders, beginning with the oldest, will go in single file to the place where the Sacristan has prepared a cross for their adoration. They will act with respect and devotion, keeping their hands joined and making a deep curtsy before and after they pray.

19. They will say the Stations of the Cross after the midday meal. Each class will go in turn. The class will begin the Stations after the nuns have already said the first two or three Stations. The boarders will march in the same order used for processions. At each Station, they will say the same prayers as the nuns, or others that they have been prescribed.

20. On Holy Saturday morning, they will go to church and say their prayers as on the preceding days. Then they will have breakfast. During the reading of the Prophets,[57] the boarders may say some of the Stations of the Cross in the way explained in the preceding paragraph, or the mistress can keep them busy with some other devotional exercise such as speaking to them about the upcoming feast day.

21. They will be present at the litanies and mass, after which they will have their midday meal.

---

55. Washing of the feet on Holy Thursday.

56. Because no hosts are consecrated on Good Friday, the hosts consecrated on Holy Thursday reserved for Good Friday mass are kept on the monstrance altar. The *Règlemens* uses the French term *reposoir* (repose altar), which also designates a temporary altar. In fact, these altars were portable and used in liturgies celebrated outside of the church sanctuary, as seems to be the case here.

57. Readings from the Old Testament prophets are part of the Easter Vigil celebrated on Holy Saturday.

22. After recess, the mistress will occupy the boarders in the same way she did on Holy Thursday morning.

23. On the day before Pentecost Sunday, the boarders will hear the low mass if it is said at the usual time in the morning. If not, they will go to church and pray for half an hour.

24. From 8:15 until 9:30 a.m., they will do the usual classwork, except for handwriting.

25. They will then recite the litanies and hear high mass.

26. On Pentecost Sunday and the two following days, they will attend terce.[58]

27. On the feast of Corpus Christi and during its octave, they will be present at the Exposition of the Blessed Sacrament in the morning and evening. Every day at 10:00 a.m., each boarder will silently say the Litany of the Virgin Mary in front of the Blessed Sacrament. On feast days, they will spend fifteen minutes in prayer to God after recess. On regular days, they will say vespers at the usual time.

28. They will follow this schedule at all times that the Blessed Sacrament is exposed, with this exception: they will not attend the *Salut*[59] if it takes place too early in the morning or too late at night, as sometimes happens with the Forty Hours Devotion.[60]

II.

Observances for the Boarders' First Communion

1. If it is at all possible, the boarders who receive the sacrament of Holy Communion for the first time will wear a dress of white cloth and a head covering and a sash of white taffeta.

2. Before the midday meal or after recess, when the boarders are all together, the mistress will have those who have made their First Communion

58. The third hour of the Divine Office, associated with 9:00 a.m., when the Holy Spirit descended on the Apostles on Pentecost.

59. The Petit Robert defines *Salut* as the Roman Catholic ceremony "qui comprend l'exposition du saint sacrement, certains chants, une bénédiction" (ceremony that includes the exposition of the Blessed Sacrament, certain hymns, and a benediction). "Salut," *Le Petit Robert* (Paris: Dictionnaires Le Robert, 1967).

60. "A devotion in which continuous prayer is made for forty hours before the Blessed Sacrament exposed" ("Forty Hours Devotion," *Catholic Encyclopedia*, vol. F, accessed June 18, 2020, https://www.newadvent.org/cathen/06151a.htm).

stand in the middle of the assembly and form two rows. The Mother Superior and some of the nuns will join them. One of the nuns will lead the others in singing the psalm *Dominus regit me.* When the psalm is finished, the same nun will sing the antiphon *O sacrum convivium.* Then the Mother Superior will say the verse *Panem de caelo* and the prayer *Deus qui nobis sub Sacramento,* etc.[61]

3. After this, the assembled boarders will sing a communion hymn or a hymn of celebration. During this singing, those who have just made their First Communion will embrace each other and then embrace the other boarders who have already made their First Communion. Finally, they will kneel and ask the Mother Superior for her blessing.

4. On that day, they will take their meals at a separate table with the General Mistress. In place of the grace before and after meals, they may sing the *Benedicite*[62] and Psalm 117, *Laudate, Domine, omnes gentes.*[63]

III.

How the Boarders Can Honor the Patron Saints of Their Class

1. The boarders in every class have permission to celebrate the feast of their patron saint by holding a ceremony with hymns and prayers or to chant vespers in plainsong in the oratory or in the classroom that has been prepared for such a celebration. Any nuns or other boarders who have a special devotion to this saint may attend the ceremony, which will normally take place after recess. It is not necessary to hold the celebration on the exact saint's day. If there is a cause for delay, it can take place within the octave of the saint's day. In that case, the older girls can also hold a brief prayer service on the actual feast day.

2. The younger boarders should pray briefly or chant a short version of vespers with only two hymns, *Dixit Dominus*[64] and *Laudate, Dominum, omnes gentes.*[65] If they wish to have a change from the usual ceremony, they may have a procession.

61. Psalm 23 is the well-known "The Lord is my shepherd." The antiphon *O sacrum convivium* (O sacred banquet) is associated with communion. *Panem de caelo* (Bread from Heaven) is sung at the end of the benediction hymn *Tantum ergo. Deus qui nobis sub Sacramento* (O God, who in this wonderful sacrament) is a prayer said after the *Tantum ergo.*

62. The *benedicite* is a variant of grace sung before or after meals.

63. Praise God, All People.

64. Psalm 109.

65. This is the first line of Psalm 117 in Latin.

3. The boarders may also sing the Litany of the Virgin Mary or chant the *Benedicite* and grace before and after meals.

4. If the school itself has a patron saint, all the boarders will come together as a choir and sing vespers in the church or in another of the school's oratories that has an altar erected in the patron's honor. In addition to vespers, they will sing the Litany of the Virgin Mary.

5. The Mother Superior will assign a nun to go to each class before the patron's feast day and teach the boarders what to sing if the Class Mistress cannot do so. She will only teach the boarders things they can easily retain so she does not waste class time.

6. Boarders are excused from their reading, writing, and needlework lessons on the feast day of their class patron. All boarders are excused from classwork on the feast day of the school's patron.

IV.

Half-Day and Full-Day Holidays

1. The boarders are exempt from writing, reading, needlework, and catechism lessons on the afternoons of the days before Kings' Day and the Thursday before Quinquagesima Sunday,[66] as well as all day on the Monday and Tuesday following Quinquagesima Sunday, on the day when the nuns renew their vows, the day of a nun's profession, or the afternoon of a day when a vesture takes place. The Mother Superior may also declare other holidays if circumstances call for them.

CHAPTER FIFTEEN

Regulations for the Boarders

1. The boarders will devote themselves entirely to the service of God, loving and honoring Him with their whole heart. They will also obey their mistresses.

2. They will be diligent in using the time their parents have given them to learn. Although their main goal is to become good Christian women, they

---

66. King's Day, or Twelfth Night, is January 6. Quinquagesima Sunday is the Sunday before Ash Wednesday.

must also try to become knowledgeable and well trained in all of the skills girls must know.

3. As soon as they awaken, they will say the morning prayers prescribed in their prayer book.[67] Once they have gotten out of bed, they will adore God and then wish their mistresses good day.

4. As they get dressed, they will say the prayers prescribed in their prayer book.

5. They will get dressed promptly so they can be ready for the prayers before mass. So that they don't waste time, as they dress they will only ask for things they need and do so in a quiet voice. They will do the same in the evening when they undress, taking care to keep their chests covered modestly.

6. Once they are dressed and have folded and put away their nightclothes, they will rinse their mouths and wash their hands.

7. They will attend mass with attention and devotion, as they have been taught to do.

8. On Sundays and feast days, when they spend more time in church, they will say, in addition to the Holy Rosary and the Office of the Blessed Virgin Mary, a few prayers for their family members, both living and dead, such as the seven penitential psalms, the Office for the Dead, the Litany of the Saints, etc. When they go to vespers, they can bring a pious book to read after they have said the Vespers of the Virgin and one other prayer. On these days, if there is no sermon, they will spend half an hour after the midday meal in pious readings or performing some other pious exercise that their mistress has assigned them.

9. They will develop a deep devotion to the Blessed Virgin Mary. They will beseech her to protect them and ask her to obtain from her dear Son, Jesus Christ, the grace for them to avoid mortal sin. In her honor, they will say the rosary and the Litany of the Virgin Mary every day, and they will do so attentively. The older boarders who can read will also say the Office of the Virgin.

10. They will also make their devotions to their guardian angels, never missing a day without praying to this angel morning and night. On the day when the Feast of the Guardian Angels occurs, they will ask permission to attend vespers.[68]

67. The boarders' prayer book contained common prayers, such as the grace before and after meals and acts of faith, hope, and charity.
68. This feast day was authorized by Pope Paul V in 1608 and is celebrated on October 2.

11. They will receive the sacrament of Penance often. They will confess their sins humbly, with the desire to make amends, always remembering that our salvation depends on making a good confession. Those boarders who have not yet made their First Communion will go to confession once a month or every six weeks.

12. A week before the principal feast days of our Lord, the Blessed Virgin, and the saints and before the first Sunday of every month, those boarders who have already made their First Communion will humbly ask their Class Mistress for permission to receive Holy Communion. They will acknowledge the esteem in which they hold such a great good and try to prepare to receive the sacrament reverently, in the way they have been taught. If the General Mistress comes into their classroom around the time of one of the feast days, the entire class will ask her for permission to receive communion.

13. On the last day of every month, the boarders from each class will draw a slip of paper from a container on which is written the name of a saint. This saint will be the girl's patron for the upcoming month. A ceremony will take place in the following manner: the boarders will assemble in the oratory and invoke the Holy Spirit by saying the *Veni, Creator spiritu.*[69] Once they have drawn their patron's name, they will say the antiphon *Sancti dei omnes,*[70] etc. They will then read about their saint's life, taking care to note his or her virtues so as to practice one of them during the month. They will ask their saint to intercede with our Lord on their behalf that He may grant them grace. On their saint's feast day, they will ask permission to leave class and attend vespers.

14. Before beginning their morning devotions and lessons, they will make the Direction of Intention[71] by offering every action of their day to Christ and saying the prayers designed for this intention.

15. They will memorize their prayers and catechism text in the proper time.

16. Every week, one of the boarders will be chosen to lead the others in the common prayers that are said aloud. She will be chosen according to her rank in class. Only a boarder from the higher classes will be chosen to read aloud during meals. A different girl will be chosen for this reading every day.

17. While the boarders reside in the convent, they will consider the teaching nuns their mothers, because these nuns do indeed take the place of their

---

69. "Come, Creator Spirit."

70. "All you Saints of Heaven" is an antiphon, that is, a prayer sung by two groups that alternate verses.

71. A short prayer attributed to Saint François de Sales said immediately upon awakening in the morning.

real mothers. The boarders will respect these nuns and obey them in all things. They will accept in a positive spirit any advice or reprimand as proof that the nuns have their best interests at heart.

18. Whenever the boarders are assembled, when a mistress arrives, they will stand and greet her and remain standing until she is seated. Should another nun come in unexpectedly, they will rise, curtsy, but then sit down immediately, unless it is an older nun.[72]

19. They will act respectfully toward all nuns. They will greet them whenever they meet and stand aside in doorways to let them pass, as courtesy requires. Whenever a nun teaches them something or does a favor, they will thank her humbly and sincerely.

20. They will address the professed Choir Nuns, even those who work in the novitiate, as "Mother" and the novices who have not yet professed and the Converse Nuns as "Sister."

21. The boarders will treat each other with civility, gentleness, and charity. They will address each other as "Sister" or "Friend."

22. They will train themselves to converse clearly and sensibly, especially when they speak with guests in the parlor. They will receive the people who come to see them courteously and humbly thank them for their visit. They will speak clearly so that the nun who accompanies them to the parlor can understand what they are saying. They will take care not to get too close to the wire netting that separates them from their visitor.

23. They will stand up straight and walk gracefully, without excessive movements of the head or hands when they are talking. They will take care to keep their clothes clean, to avoid damaging their clothes, to always wear gloves as well as masks[73] and hats when they go into the school courtyard or garden.

24. They will ask nothing of anyone who visits them in the parlor, unless they have permission from the General Mistress to do so. They will show the General Mistress anything they receive from a visitor, especially books and letters. They will not ask a visitor to mail any letters for them that the General Mistress has not seen first. They will also show either the General Mistress or the Bursar any clothes they have been given or that they are sending back to their family. As for their personal linen, they should notify the Linen Mistress when they receive any or send any back.

72. In this case, the boarders remain standing as a sign of respect to the older nun.
73. Cloth masks were worn as protection from the sun.

25. They will not give away or cut into pieces any old clothes without the permission of the General Mistress, nor will they lend clothes to each other without permission of the Class Mistress.

26. Because a good upbringing requires that girls know something about managing a household, the older boarders will take care of their own personal linen, always keeping it clean and neatly put away in their clothes chest. They will fold the linen after it has been washed and do any necessary mending. During the winter, they will go one at a time to the Linen Mistress's rooms and help her iron their collars and neckerchiefs. Whenever they receive new linen, they will help the Linen Mistress mark it for identification.

27. They will also mend their clothing from time to time, make their own beds, and clean their combs and brushes.

28. Every week, one of them will be assigned to set the table before meals with napkins, cups, and spoons. After the meal, she will remove the napkins and fold them neatly into a pile.

29. The boarders will take turns at caring for class supplies, that is, books, needlework, jetons, etc. The mistress will establish the order in which the boarders take turns.

30. They will go into church, the school oratory, as well as into their class-rooms, in a calm and orderly manner, taking care not to make noise or speak in a loud voice when they are near the church, the parlors, or other places of communal use. They will observe the same behavior in the classroom so that lessons can proceed smoothly. During writing, arithmetic, and spelling classes, they will only speak when it is necessary. On the days when their class does not have instruction in catechism, they will not make any noise that could distract those classes that are studying catechism.

31. They will always act politely during meals, humbly thanking those who serve them for everything. They will never show displeasure at what they are given to eat because nothing is more unbecoming of a girl of high birth or good upbringing. They will only talk at meals to ask, in a low voice, for something they need, and they will do so using terms of supplication, as good manners require.

32. When they finish their meal and leave the table, they will say grace and then clean their mouths. Afterward, they will go out to recess quietly, making sure to stay within the mistress's sight. They may play checkers, chess, badminton, and other such games. On the days they receive communion, they should limit their entertainment to hearing pious speeches.

33. They will not leave the classroom or any other place where they are assembled without the mistress's permission. They are expressly forbidden to go into any of the nuns' quarters, such as the nuns' dormitory, refectory, chapter room, etc., under any pretext whatsoever. However, on extraordinary holidays, the boarders may receive permission to enter the nuns' residence.

34. They will not eat anything between their four daily meals, because eating between meals is contrary to good etiquette and harmful to the health. They may not pick the fruit growing in the convent garden.

35. In winter, they will arrange their hair for the night during the evening recess. They will do the same on those evenings when they attend matins, putting on their taffeta nightcaps before they enter church.

36. In winter, they will also withdraw to their rooms before 7:00 p.m. to say their prayers and examine their conscience according to the formula written in their prayer book.

37. Before they get into bed, they will adore God as prescribed in their prayer book, make the Sign of the Cross with holy water, and, having wished their mistress good night, get in bed without making a fuss and try to think good thoughts as they fall asleep.

SECOND PART
Day Pupils

CHAPTER ONE
The General Order of Classes

1. The day pupils will be divided into several classes, depending on the number of pupils and the ability of the school building to accommodate several classrooms.

2. Each class will have a patron saint, and in each classroom there will be some type of altar covered with a fitted mat. If this is not possible, the classroom should at least have a painting or some other image of the patron saint.

3. A General Mistress will be in charge of all the classes, and each class will have its own two Class Mistresses, who will take turns weekly teaching catechism and all the other subjects prescribed by the regulations. If possible, the higher classes will have, in addition to the Class Mistresses, a nun to teach the reading of handwritten letters as well as counting and arithmetic. This nun may replace a Class Mistress in catechism and other subjects if the mistress is absent.

4. In addition, there will be one or two mistresses to teach writing to all the classes. If there are enough nuns in the convent, a few may be selected to teach needlework.

5. Because the day pupils are usually quite numerous, each class may be further divided into several groups, with a maximum of ten girls in each group. Authority over each group will be given to one or two exceptionally

well-behaved and knowledgeable pupils called *dixainières*.[74] A later chapter will list their duties.

6. The day pupils will usually have four hours of instruction a day, one and one-half hours in the morning and two and one-half hours in the afternoon.

7. Classes will not take place on Saturday afternoon, unless there have been several feast days that week. There will be no classes on the days before the major feast days, that is, the feasts of the Circumcision, Holy Trinity, Conception, Nativity, and the Purification of the Blessed Virgin Mary, or on the vigils of the feasts of the apostles, when the teachers are required to fast.

8. The weekly half-day will be moved from Saturday to another day of the week if pupils have more need of free time on that day to fulfill their obligations to their family. On half-days, pupils will have class for two hours and fifteen minutes in the morning. In addition, there will be no class on the afternoon of the Thursday preceding Quinquagesima Sunday or on the following Monday or Tuesday, the morning of Ash Wednesday, from the afternoon of Wednesday of Holy Week until the day after the end of Easter feast days, the mornings of Monday and Tuesday and all day Wednesday of Rogations Week, and the day before Pentecost; or when a girl becomes a novice or makes her profession; or if there is a funeral or any such occasion that requires the nuns to be present.

9. Day pupils will have three weeks of vacation in autumn or in another season, depending on what is customary in their region and what is most convenient.

10. There will be a little bell in that part of the convent where the day school is located that rings to signal when it is time for the day pupils to enter and leave the building. The bell will also signal the end of catechism lesson.

CHAPTER TWO

The General Mistress of the Day School

1. The General Mistress will be zealous in the instruction of youth and in promoting the progress of the day pupils, as much in the acquisition of virtue and piety as in everything they study.

---

74. There is no exact translation for this term, which means "a girl in charge of about ten others."

2. She will keep an eye on the Class Mistresses to be sure that they fulfill their duty. She will try to ensure that the mistresses maintain good relationships among themselves and help them preserve the authority they have over their pupils. She will never correct a mistress or show her displeasure with a mistress while pupils are present but, rather, defer these observations to another time when she can accompany her criticism with the necessary good advice.

3. She will assiduously open the door at exactly the required time to allow the pupils to enter and leave the school building. She will remain at the door whenever it is open, taking care that no one who should not be there slips in. To do this, she will keep her veil lifted above her eyes. Nor will she take time from this duty to speak to anyone who is not a pupil, nun, or priest, but, rather, she will close the door as soon as the pupils have come in or gone out.

4. She will make certain that there is never any disorderly behavior in the area where the pupils gather before entering the school. If necessary, she will obtain the help of the convent gatekeeper or some other person who can remain in the assembly area to keep the pupils in order. Or she can entrust the authority and the means to keep order to one of the older day pupils who is exceptionally mature.

5. She will also keep an eye on the pupils as they enter and leave to make sure they are not disorderly or noisy. She will make a note of any missing pupil and inquire as soon as possible the reason for this absence. She will do her best to impress upon the pupils the need to be punctual, and she has the right to punish or dismiss any pupil who is habitually tardy without a legitimate reason.

6. When, in spite of the General Mistress's best efforts, there are several pupils who do not arrive on time to enter the building with the others, the General Mistress, with the consent of the Mother Superior, will open the door a second time to admit these pupils. This is necessary to ward off any problems that could arise if the girls wandered about unsupervised for a long time.

7. If the weather is bad, the General Mistress will open the building later so the pupils have an easier time getting to school. On the afternoons of the seasons when the days are shorter, she will allow the pupils to leave earlier so they can get home safely.

8. When a girl asks to be educated in the day school, before she can be admitted, the General Mistress will make her acquaintance in the parlor, find out her age, where she lives, if her parents are able and willing to send her to school every day at the appointed time, and if they will make the girl

practice everything she learns in school concerning piety. The parents must ensure that the girl says her prayers in the morning and evening, goes to mass on Sundays and holy days of obligation, and goes to confession during major feast days.

9. The General Mistress will not admit any girl who does not know the letters of the alphabet and how to assemble the letters into simple words. The only exception is an older girl who has come only to receive religious instruction.

10. She will not admit any girl, especially in the case of older girls, if she cannot be assured by someone well acquainted with the family that the parents or guardians are of good moral character. She will not admit any girl who is eighteen years old or older without the permission of the Mother Superior.

11. She will keep a book in which she records the name of every girl admitted to the day school, her age, the occupation of her parents, and where she resides.

12. After she has decided which girls to admit, she will normally wait until the beginning of the next month to let them enter. She will distribute them among the different classes according to their ages and the number of pupils already in each class.

13. In the parlor, she will conduct herself with the parents of her pupils in a way that befits the parents' condition.[75] She will speak succinctly and only about subjects regarding her office. She will keep her veil slightly lowered over her eyes.

14. She will never ask the pupils to carry messages for her without the express permission of the Mother Superior unless such a message pertains to her work; that is, to send for a pupil's parents, to find out why a pupil is absent, etc.

15. She will never receive any letters or anything else brought to the door of the day school, except for notes explaining a pupil's absence or asking that a pupil be excused from school. She will show such notes to the nun who opens and closes the door. This nun must be present when she receives such notes.

16. She will change the girls serving as *dixainières* every three or four months. She will do this after conferring with the Class Mistresses to learn which girls are most capable. She will write down their names, then go into the classrooms, give the names of those she has chosen, and exhort them to acquit

---

75. Here *condition* probably refers to the parent's educational level. Many parents of day pupils were undoubtedly illiterate.

themselves honorably of their duties. Normally, she will give some small reward to those who are leaving their posts. If it is difficult to find enough capable girls as replacements, the current *dixainières* may continue to serve longer.

17. She will go into the classes every two or three months to see how the pupils are progressing in their study of Christian doctrine, reading, and writing. Once or twice a year, she will have their regulations read to the day pupils.

18. When the lower classes are too full, she may move some pupils up to the higher classes. She will take into account the pupil's age and ability when doing so.

19. Three or four times a year, with the Mother Superior's permission, she will ask confessors to come to the school to hear the day pupils' confessions if the priest who serves as confessor to the convent cannot do this. When she knows the day and time of the confessors' arrival, she will inform the Class Mistresses so they can prepare their pupils.

20. Once the confessors have arrived, the General Mistress will lead the pupils out of the classroom and divide those who have completed their preparation into groups. She will work with each class separately. She will have one of the older girls lead the groups into church. In this way, the confessors will never have to wait. Once most of the pupils in a group have confessed, one of them will notify the girl in charge of the next group so that those who have finished can return to class and the next group can come into church.

21. She will give each confessor a box in which he can put the names of those who have been to confession.

22. When there are enough pupils ready to make their First Communion, she will follow the method of preparation given in chapter five of the first part. She will find out from the parents if they wish their daughters to receive the sacrament and if their parish priest is in agreement. What is said in chapter five, namely, that either the General Mistress or the Class Mistress may prepare the boarders for the sacrament, is applicable to the day pupils.

23. The General Mistress will find out when the bishop is bestowing the sacrament of Confirmation and inform the Class Mistresses so they can prepare the pupils to receive the sacrament. If a pupil's parents cannot take her to the church where the bishop is conducting the ceremony, the General Mistress will ask the Gatekeeper, or some other reliable person, to take the pupil to this church.

24. With the permission of the Mother Superior, she will keep any money the day pupils give her to buy ink, pens, brooms, and any other class supplies.

She will make sure that those pupils who have the means to do so will contribute something, however small the sum. For example, those pupils who can write should give two or three *sous* a year for pens and ink. Everyone, except those who are too poor, should contribute one *sou* a month for the class's little necessities. The General Mistress will explain this requirement to parents when she admits a girl to the day school. She will also tell the parents to send wood to heat the school in winter. It goes without saying that such requests will only be made in those communities where the parents will neither be offended by the request nor derive a sense of superiority from them. In those regions where less than a *sou* will suffice to pay for the above-mentioned monthly expenses, the General Mistress will ask for less money.

25. This money may not be used for any other purpose. If any money is left over, it will serve to decorate the class oratory, as the Mother Superior has ordered, and to purchase rosaries, pictures, cloth to make *Agnus Dei*,[76] etc., or for rewards given by the Class Mistress. However, the General Mistress may not spend more than two or three *écu* a year for the expenses of two or three classes. As for the prizes for which she is responsible as overseer of the entire school, she should not spend more than one *écu* per year. She will distribute the money for class ornaments, holy objects, and class rewards to the Class Mistresses once a year, giving more or fewer objects depending on the number of pupils in each class.

26. If it is more convenient for the pupils, the General Mistress may purchase the Latin and French books used in class, as well as the catechisms, and writing paper. She must sell them to the pupils for the same amount she paid. She will also furnish the Writing Mistress with paper, ink, and penknives.

27. She will ask the Gatekeeper to buy all these supplies. She will never ask a pupil to make any purchases without the permission of the Mother Superior.

CHAPTER THREE
The Class Mistresses of the Day Pupils

1. The nuns who have been chosen to teach day pupils should carry out their work lovingly, all the more so because this work allows them to imitate

---

76. The Agnus Dei is normally a wax disk, but this paragraph suggests that the Agnus Dei was made of cloth rather than wax.

more closely the Son of God, whose central mission, during His time on earth, was to teach the poor and ignorant. They must be insistent in their prayers to the Holy Spirit for the grace to perform their duties with the zeal, charity, patience, and kindness that Christ exemplified.

2. In each class, two Class Mistresses will have the principal care of the pupils. The mistress *en semaine* will help the pupils learn their prayers and teach them reading in the morning and catechism in the afternoon. The other mistress will teach reading in the afternoon and help the pupils examine their conscience unless it is more practical for the mistress *en semaine* to do so.

3. On half-days, when the pupils are only in school in the morning, the mistress *en semaine* will teach catechism at the most convenient time, and the other mistress will teach reading.

4. The mistress who is not conducting the reading lesson will read individually with the least advanced girls. If there is time, she will teach some of these girls to read manuscript and arithmetic, unless there is another nun who teaches these subjects.

5. The method for teaching reading in the day school is the same as that given in the first part, chapter three, paragraph 15, on the Class Mistresses of the boarders. When a pupil is called upon to read, she will stand and read so that she can be heard more clearly. She will read two or three lines of verse or five or six lines of prose, depending on the number of pupils and amount of time available.

6. The mistresses will arrive punctually at the prescribed hour. The mistress *en semaine* will always be in the classroom before the pupils enter.

7. They will devote all class time to the pupils' benefit, never allowing themselves to be distracted from teaching. They will be even more careful not to waste time speaking to each other during the time assigned for instruction. They should put off all conversations until later for the good of the pupils.

8. They will teach catechism using the method prescribed in the first part, in the chapter on the Class Mistresses of the boarding school (chapter four, paragraph 1). Before the important feast days, they will talk during catechism lesson about the remarkable things done by Our Lord, the Blessed Virgin, and the saints. They will also discuss the most significant religious ceremonies, such as the liturgy of Ash Wednesday or Palm Sunday.

9. Because their main duty is to form the pupils in piety and Christian virtue, they will take special care in this teaching and give pupils individual attention. When a girl enters the day school, the lead mistress will ask her

THREE CENTURIES OF GIRLS' EDUCATION

to offer herself to God in the way explained in the first part, chapter four, paragraph 5. This mistress will teach the new pupil the principal doctrines of the Christian faith and religion and the correct way to pray to God in the morning, to hear mass, and to examine her conscience before she goes to bed. This mistress will then place the girl in the charge of the *dixainière*, who will teach the girl her prayers and go over the catechism text with her.

10. When she is not *en semaine*, the First Class Mistress will normally appoint someone to ascertain what the new pupil has learned about faith and doctrine while the other pupils say their morning prayers. The Second Mistress will do the same during morning prayers if the First Mistress directs her to do so.

11. The Class Mistresses will have the day pupils say the prayers they have learned often so they do not forget them. The mistresses can have the pupils pray if any time remains after the reading lesson. One pupil will recite the prayers aloud while the others listen attentively.

12. The mistresses will have the day pupils confess their sins in their parish churches at Easter and the other important holy days of the year in addition to the three or four times a year they go to confession in the convent church. The pupils will prepare themselves in the manner described in the first part, chapter four, paragraph 2. The First Mistress will speak privately with those pupils who are less knowledgeable or who need more care, observing the advice given in the same chapter, paragraphs 3 and 4. If there are too many pupils for her to speak to them all, she may ask the Second Mistress to help her.

13. On the days when the day pupils confess in the convent, they will be separated into groups of no more than eighteen or twenty. They will go to the oratory or some other convenient place to examine their conscience. The lead mistress will say aloud the main sins that the pupils must consider, pausing now and then to give the girls ample time to examine themselves. After this, she will encourage them to formulate their own acts of contrition while giving them an example to imitate. Finally, she will hand each girl a slip of paper on which her name is written. The girl will give the paper to the confessor so that he can keep track of which girls have been to confession.

14. If there is any day pupil who has exceptional difficulty going to confession and needs individual help, the First Mistress will inform the General Mistress, who will, in turn, alert the confessor and put a special mark by the girl's name so the confessor can recognize the girl.

15. The First Mistress will alert the General Mistress when it is time for the day pupils to go to confession.

16. The Class Mistresses will inform the day pupils that they may not take communion without having first asked permission. In this way, the mistresses can prepare the girls to receive the sacrament when they judge it appropriate to do so. In all cases, the mistresses must obtain the authorization of the General Mistress. They must also take care not to offend the priests who serve as confessors or spiritual directors.

17. They will inform the General Mistress when some of the day pupils are ready to make their First Communion. The mistress in charge of preparing the girls to receive the sacrament will follow, as closely as possible, the method prescribed for the boarders in the first part, chapter five.

18. They will prepare the day pupils for Confirmation in this way: when the General Mistress has told the mistresses the day the bishop has selected for Confirmation, they will prepare the day pupils as described in the first part, chapter four, paragraph 4. They will make sure that the pupils go to confession on the previous day and that all pupils have a clean, white headband for the ceremony. Because the above-mentioned chapter of the first part is cited frequently in these regulations for the day pupils, the mistresses should keep a copy of the chapter available.

19. When a day pupil decides to withdraw from the school, the First Mistress will speak to her in private, urging her to live a good Christian life and always to think about what she must do to gain eternal life.

20. The mistresses will keep to the exact order of classes established in the regulations. They will change nothing in the prayers prescribed for the day pupils.

21. They will have the day pupils read their regulations twice a year, in addition to the one or two times the General Mistress reads them to the class. The mistresses can have the *dixainières* read the regulations more often if this helps them better carry out their duties.

22. The Class Mistresses will conduct themselves with great patience and charity in their dealings with all of their pupils. They will take delight in helping the pupils make progress in everything they study, encouraging them to learn and to become virtuous. They can even give little rewards furnished by the General Mistress, as prescribed in these regulations, to encourage the ones who work the hardest. They will take care not to place pupils from wealthier families too close to the ones who are poor and dirty, lest the wealth-

ier pupils find the poorer ones distasteful. However, the Class Mistresses must separate the rich from the poor discreetly, lest the poor girls feel they are being scorned. At all times, the Class Mistresses will show the same respect and affection to all pupils, without regard to a pupil's condition.

23. They will have a list of the names of all the pupils in their classes so they can carefully note those who are absent. They will inquire into the cause of this absence immediately and give the General Mistress the names of those who are habitually absent.

24. They will also report any notable incidents of bad behavior to the General Mistress so she can correct the pupils. They should only rarely punish a pupil whose behavior has been reported by another pupil. They will thus prevent animosities from arising among the pupils themselves and perhaps even among the pupils' parents. Such problems come about when girls are encouraged to inform on one another.

25. In matters of minor misconduct, such as talking in class, neglecting studies, or being rude to classmates, if the Class Mistress has warned a pupil and the pupil refuses to correct her behavior, the mistress should cause the pupil some slight embarrassment like making her sit at the back of the class, or away from the other pupils, or stand for a short time, etc.

26. The Class Mistress will not allow pupils to do each other's assignments or to make any deals with their classmates concerning their schoolwork.

27. The Class Mistresses will not take presents from pupils. They will never use a pupil to send a message or request to someone outside of the convent. They will not question pupils about the latest news or engage in small talk. They will not even allow the pupils to bring up such idle subjects during private conversations, lest they waste time better spent in instruction.

28. They will ensure that the area of the convent used for the day school is always kept neat and clean. This is especially necessary for the classrooms, which should be swept every day. The Class Mistress can either assign the sweeping to one or two pupils, who can help each other if necessary, or she can pay someone to sweep regularly. The paid cleaner may be one of the poor pupils. In this case, the girl will remain in the classroom after the other pupils have gone home, and then she will sweep. The mistress will leave her alone in the classroom until she has finished her work, opening the door afterward to allow her to leave.

29. The Class Mistresses will always act respectfully toward the General Mistress. They will be charitable toward one another and of one mind as they help each other in the classroom. If any little disagreements arise between them or with the General Mistress, they will not air these matters in front of the pupils. If one mistress disapproves of what the other is doing, she will wait until class is finished to reprimand the other mistress and do so kindly and delicately.

CHAPTER FOUR

The Writing Mistress

1. The Writing Mistress will divide the day pupils who are ready to write into groups. Each group of pupils will write for half an hour during the reading lesson. The mistress will keep track of the time with an hourglass.

2. With the permission of the Class Mistress, the Writing Mistress will put one pupil in charge of setting out paper and ink for the writing lesson. When the lesson is finished, this pupil will set aside those papers that require correction and put away the inkwells.

3. The Writing Mistress will always have a ready supply of sharpened feather pens so she can spend the entire class time in instruction.

4. She should address the General Mistress for all writing supplies. She will remind the pupils of the sums they are expected to contribute for pens and ink and note the names of those who have contributed.

5. For directions in teaching writing and maintaining order in the classroom, she will observe the methods given in these regulations, first part, chapter six, on the Writing Mistress of the boarding school. She will pay special attention to paragraph 7, which says that the mistress may not permit the pupils to talk to each other during the lesson, nor should she herself engage in small talk with the pupils nor allow the pupils to talk to her.

6. If there are other nuns available for teaching needlework, arithmetic, spelling, and reading handwritten letters, they will follow the methods given in the first part, chapters seven and eight, with the approval of the Mother Superior and the General Mistress, who will decide upon the practicality of such instruction.

CHAPTER FIVE
The Day Pupils

I.

1. The girls who are received into the school must understand that their primary goal—the goal for which they are admitted—is to know, love, and serve God so that they may one day share His everlasting happiness in heaven.

2. They will devote themselves to acts of piety and learn and practice everything they are taught that is necessary for their salvation, making every effort to show by their good works and the modesty of their deportment how much they love God and fear His displeasure.

3. As soon as they awaken in the morning they will give their hearts to God, saying, "My God, I give you my heart, etc." As soon as they arise from bed, they will say, "For the love of you, my sweetest Jesus, etc." These are the same prayers said by the boarders.

4. Once they are out of bed, they will sign themselves with holy water, get on their knees to adore God, and say the following prayer: "Dear God, I come to You as humbly as I know how. I confess my sins, those known and unknown. Lord, You know I am not perfect and I fall short every day of my life, but I want to take time out to say thank You for Your mercy. Thank You for my health, my family, and my friends, the roof over my head, the food on my table, and everything I have. Amen."[77] They will then commend themselves to the Blessed Virgin and to their guardian angel, saying the prayers: "O Most Holy Virgin, after God most powerful, etc." and "Holy Angel of God, my guardian dear, etc." On the days when they have no class, they will then say the prayer used in the classroom.

5. They will attend mass devoutly every day, if possible, or at least on Sundays and feast days. During mass, they will behave as they have been taught to do, neither talking nor turning their head nor performing any other irreverent act.

6. They will demonstrate the same piety every time they enter a church, not only for mass but when they hear vespers or the priest's sermon. They

---

77. The French title of this prayer is *Humblement prosterné, Seigneur* (see *Chants d'espérance*, Chant Chorale et Groupe app, accessed December 22, 2021, http://chant.rezo509.com/mobile/MobileChantViewDetails.aspx?ID=364&tc=FR&ri=160&rwndrnd=0.541450806427747).

should attend both vespers and sermons on Sundays and feast days with their parents' permission.

7. Every night before going to bed, they will examine their conscience as they have been taught. The will commend themselves to God, saying their night prayers and a *De profundis*[78] for the souls in purgatory.

8. Before getting into bed, they will sign themselves with holy water and adore God, saying the prayer "My God, my lord and my father, etc." As they get into bed, they will say, "In Your name and for You, my God, give me grace, etc." Then they will give their hearts to God as they did in the morning and try to fall asleep while thinking good thoughts.

9. They must be especially devoted to the Virgin Mary and imitate her virtues so that she will be their mother and advocate and take them into her holy protection. Every day, they will say the rosary in her honor or at least the Little Crown of twelve *aves*[79] and the Litany of the Virgin.

10. They must also be greatly devoted to their guardian angels and to the saints whose names they bear. They should pray to their angel and saint at least every morning and evening.

11. They will always be obedient to their mothers and fathers or to the guardians who take their parents' place, honoring and serving them as God commands and trying never to cause them displeasure either by their words or actions.

12. They will go to confession every month, or at least before every important feast day. Those who wish to receive communion will not approach the sacred altar without first asking the permission of their confessor or their Class Mistresses. They will humbly ask their mistresses to teach them how to prepare themselves so that they may be worthy to receive the sacrament.

II.

The Order Day Pupils Must Observe
on the Days When They Come to Class

1. They will gather in the exterior assembly room fifteen minutes before the school doors are opened. When they enter the room, they will go to their

---

78. Psalm 129, one of the seven penitential psalms.

79. "The 'Little Crown of the Blessed Virgin Mary' is a chaplet recited in honor of the 12 stars in Our Lady's heavenly crown, as mentioned in Revelation 11:19–12:1." Catholic Company, accessed December 23, 2021, https://www.catholiccompany.com/content/little-crown-virgin-mary.

assigned seats without making noise, or playing, arguing, or engaging in any other disorderly behavior. They will use this time to eat breakfast or learn their prayers or study catechism. They will always obey whoever is in charge of them while they are in this area.

2. When the school doors are opened, the pupils will enter two by two. Each class will enter separately, as will each group of ten into which the class is divided. The *dixainière* will follow her group. As they enter, the pupils will curtsy to the nuns who open the doors and enter their classrooms in the same ranks without talking on their way.

3. As they enter the classroom, they will curtsy to the Class Mistress and take their seats on the benches until the mistress tells them to rise for prayer.

4. Before beginning, the entire class will turn toward the painting or image on the class oratory, curtsy, then kneel. The mistress *en semaine*, speaking aloud, will lead the class in saying *In nomine patris*, etc.,[80] and "My Lord and my God, in union with your great purity, etc." Then the mistress will say all of the daily prayers and the prayer to the Holy Virgin Mary that begins "O Holy Virgin, Mother of God, Queen of angels and men, etc." She will then invoke the protection of the patron saint of the class, and each *dixainière* will invoke the saint of the month for her group. The mistress officiating will conclude the prayers, saying *Omnes sancti et sanctae Dei, etc.*[81]

5. While kneeling, the pupils will say to themselves the prayers led by the mistress and will give the responses indicated in their prayer books.

6. When prayers are over, the pupils will rise together without making noise and, after curtsying toward the oratory and to their mistresses, take their seats. They will observe the same conduct in all their classes.

7. When the pupils are seated, the d*ixainières* will distribute books to their groups unless the mistress has told them to distribute the books before prayer. Once the pupils have found their place in the books, they will follow attentively and read to themselves what the mistress is reading aloud. They will remain attentive and follow the text during class recitation so that they always know where the preceding pupil has stopped and be ready when they are called upon to read.

8. When the more advanced pupils have finished reading, they may learn to read handwritten letters or to count and do arithmetic. The mistress may

80. In making the sign of the cross.
81. The Litany of the Saints.

also give permission to those pupils who are the best readers and who study most diligently to work on needlework, etc., if they have read sufficiently.

9. Those pupils who are learning handwriting will write for one half-hour every day, either in the morning or afternoon. When the Writing Mistress summons these pupils, they will rise, curtsy to the Class Mistress, and go to the writing room calmly, without making noise, and sit at the place where the paper they will use has been placed. Before beginning to write, they will make the Sign of the Cross. At the end of the half-hour, the Writing Mistress will tell them to put away their work. They will curtsy to her, then go back to their classroom and continue reading.

10. They will leave the school building in the same order in which they entered. They will take care not to run in the street or appear frivolous or scatterbrained because these behaviors are unbecoming of a girl educated in piety. Rather, they will go home quietly without stopping along the way.

11. When they return to school after their midday meal, they will arrive in the outside assembly room before the starting time of afternoon classes and will behave in the same way they do in the morning. Once they have entered the classroom, they will say the Litany of the Blessed Virgin, unless they have already said it in the morning, then a prayer for their intentions, such as "O My God, I offer You this work, etc.," and, finally an antiphon such as *Veni Sancte*, etc., *Monstra te*, etc., or *Angele Dei*,[82] etc.

12. During catechism lesson, the pupils will listen attentively in order to retain what they have learned. Afterward, if they have any questions, one pupil at a time will ask. This will avoid everyone speaking at the same time. If the Mother Superior and the General Mistress deem it appropriate, the reading lesson will take place first, then catechism, then the questions and answers.

13. At the beginning of catechism lesson, the *dixainière* whose group has been called upon to recite the text will stand near the mistress and question her classmates. Afterward, she will go back to her seat.

14. At the end of catechism, the pupils will kneel, and the officiating mistress will say *Sit nomen Domini benedictum*,[83] etc. Then the *dixainières* will hand out the reading books, and the reading lesson will take place as in the morning.

---

82. *Veni Sancte*, prayer to the Holy Spirit; *Monstra te*, prayer to the Virgin Mary found in the hymn *Ave Maris Stella; Angele Dei*, prayer to the guardian angel.

83. The first words of the traditional episcopal blessing, used here instead of the more common *Dominus vobiscum* (The Lord be with you).

15. When the reading is over, fifteen minutes before the end of the school day, the pupils will examine their conscience using the formula found in their prayer books and then make an act of contrition. The officiating mistress will say *Benedicta sit Sancta,*[84] *Pater noster, Ave Maria, Credo in Deum,*[85] and any other of the evening prayers.

16. When the doors are opened, the pupils will leave in the same order as they entered. The pupils appointed to help clean the classroom will be the last to leave.

17. Every week, the mistress will choose some pupils to say the prayers aloud in class. These pupils will take care to pronounce the prayers distinctly and calmly.

18. While they are in class, the day pupils will not talk, unless it is absolutely necessary. They will not eat breakfast or a snack unless they have permission to do so.

19. They will respect the *dixainière,* always doing cheerfully and promptly what she asks of them. They will treat her affectionately and learn carefully everything she teaches them.

20. The day pupils must not get angry at their *dixainière* if she corrects them or relates their mistakes to the Class Mistress. They must not blame her or say mean things to her. Rather, they should remember that she is doing her duty when she corrects them. The pupils would only be right to blame the *dixainière* if she failed in her duty to correct them.

21. If a day pupil is sick or cannot come to class for some other reason, she must ask someone to inform the General Mistress of the reason for her absence. Any day pupil who misses class without a justifiable excuse will be punished. If a pupil continues to miss class, her place will be given to someone else.

22. Every month, each group of ten pupils in every class will draw a slip of paper with the name of the saint who will be the group's patron for the month. Before drawing the patron's name, the group will say the *Veni Sancte,* etc., and after, the antiphon *Sancti Dei omnes,* etc.

23. On the feast day of the patron saint of their class, they may sing the litanies of the saints and say prayers and sing hymns in their classroom. Day pupils from other classes may attend the ceremony. Before the important feast days, individual classes may hold such ceremonies.

---

84. Prayer to the Holy Trinity.

85. *Pater noster,* the Our Father, or Lord's Prayer; *Ave Maria,* the Hail Mary; *Credo in Deum,* the Apostles' Creed.

III.
The Duties of the
Dixainières

1. It is an honor to be chosen *dixainière* to help the mistress in her teaching. This honor requires the *dixainières* to strive always to be the best behaved and most virtuous of pupils and to observe most conscientiously these regulations and obey their mistresses. Above all, they must act most charitably toward their classmates and be zealous in their instruction of catechism and prayers.

2. They will always be the first to arrive in the outside assembly room and will come to school every day without fail.

3. They will make a note of the day pupils in their group who are absent and give their names to the General Mistress as they enter the school.

4. They will take care of the books used by their group. They will put them away when the books are not in use, either on shelves or in a cabinet designed to hold them. They will separate the French books from those in Latin. They will hand the books out promptly and noiselessly in the morning and the afternoon. When the reading lesson is over, they will again put the books away.

5. They will ensure that the ten girls in their group do their work and never become disorderly. If the girls misbehave, she will point this out to them without scolding them or getting angry. If she has corrected them two or three times unsuccessfully, she will alert the mistresses. She will not exaggerate their misbehavior or cover up any actions by the pupil's friends that might have contributed to her misbehavior. The main faults that the *dixainière* should note are arguments, insults, thefts, fights, running in the streets, playing naughty games, playing with boys, making noise in the classroom, and refusing to act reasonably after being told to do so.

THE END

INDEX

Angela Merici and Her Teaching Idea (Monica), 6, 16–21

archives: Haute Garonne, 13; St. Louis, MO, ix; Ursuline Academy, ix, 2

Bellarmine, Robert, 48, 112
Bermond, Françoise de, 21–22, 26–27
boarders, 4, 8, 17, 28–44, 46–49, 74–149
Boileau, Nicolas, 12
Bonnefons, Amable, 112

Calvin, John, 46
Canevin, John, 89
Cardinal Richelieu, 48, 101, 112
Carter, Karen, 46–47
Cather, Willa, 2
Catholic Action, 82, 87
A Century of Pioneering (Heaney), 3, 6
Chervel, André, ix, 8, 43–44, 64–65, 67
choir nuns, 28, 32–33, 97, 132, 147
Christian Brothers, 52, 55, 67
Clark, Emily, 3, 5–6, 12, 22
Clark, Linda, 77
Clermont-Ferrand, 56

College of New Rochelle, 81
Company of St. Ursula, 16, 18–21, 25
Congrégation de la Mère de Dieu, 52, 66
Congrégation de la Sainte Enfance, 72
Congrégation de Marie immaculée, 73
Congregation de Paris, 5–7, 13–14, 17, 24, 28–29, 56–57, 91
Congrégation des Saints Anges, 72–73
Constitutions des religieuses de Sainte Ursule de la Congrégation de Paris, 11, 13–14, 24, 27, 29, 36, 56–57, 61, 71, 80, 95
converse nuns, 28–29, 32, 57, 76, 132, 135, 147
Council of Trent, 22–23, 46, 48, 101–102
Counsels of Angela Merici, 19–22
Counter-Reformation, 7–9, 16, 22, 24–27, 46, 99, 102

Daniélou, Madeleine, 84
day pupils, 28–29, 31, 35–36, 38–40, 42, 49, 61–62, 64, 69, 89, 94, 151–67
De l'éducation des filles (Fénelon), 16, 42
de Sales, François, 9, 24–26, 120, 146
Des règlemens communs du monastère, 13–14, 25–26, 33, 94, 102

Descartes, René, 8
devotional movement of the seventeenth
century, 24–26
dictées, 44, 62, 65, 67
Diderot, Denis, 9, 76
dignités de confiance, 75
Divine Office, 91, 115, 137–38, 140, 142
dixainières, 11, 31–32, 37–38, 41–42, 48, 60, 62,
152, 154–55, 159, 164–65, 167
Doyle, Ann Margaret, 52–55
Dupanloup, Félix, 84

Education at the Crossroads (Maritain), 83
educational reforms in France (1801–1880), 51–55
en semaine, 11, 30, 59, 104–105, 109, 113, 141,
157–58, 164
Erasmus, Desiderius, 20, 41–42
establishment of Ursulines in France, 21–24
externat, 28, 77
externes, 29, 31, 35, 39, 42, 61–62, 71

feminism and the Ursulines, 3
Fénelon, François, 16, 42, 86
Flaubert, Gustave, 10, 76–77
Forty Hours Devotion, 142
French Revolution, 7, 13, 15, 18, 51–52, 55, 65, 67

Grenade, Luis de, 120
Grew, Raymond, 51, 54–55, 64, 70

Harrington, Patrick, 51, 54–55, 64, 70
Heaney, Sr. Frances, OSU, 2–3, 6, 12, 23
Hugo, Victor, 89

Ignatius of Loyola, 9
Introduction to the Devout Life (de Sales), 9,
25–26

Jesuits, 1, 6, 9, 17, 22–23, 26–27, 52
Jules Ferry Laws, 55, 77, 81

Kane, Harnett, 2
Kersey, Shirley, 45
Keylor, William R., 78

La Princesse de Clèves (Lafayette), 9
La Religieuse (Diderot), 9, 76

Laclos, Pierre Choderlos de, 9
Lafayette, Mme de, 9
Langlois, Claude, 52
Les Liaisons dangereuses (Laclos), 9, 76
Les Misérables (Hugo), 89
literary critiques of convent education, 8–9,
75–78
Loi Camille Sée, 55
Loi Falloux, 54–55, 66, 68
Loi Guizot, 53–54, 66, 68, 70
Louis XIV, 6, 8, 15, 24, 51, 74
Louis XV, 2
Luther, Martin, 46
Lux-Sterritt, Laurence, 3, 5–6, 13, 22, 24–25
lycée, 53, 66

Machiavelli, Niccolò, 20
Madame Bovary (Flaubert), 10, 75–77
Maintenon, Mme de, 8, 15–16
Marie de Medici, 23
Maritain, Jacques, 81–83
Markham, J. David, 53, 67
Masterless Mistresses (Clark), 3, 6, 22
Merici, Angela, 1, 6–8, 16–17, 18–21, 31, 71, 79,
82–85, 89
Molière, 9
Monica, Sr. M., OSU, 6, 12, 17–25, 58, 79
Montaigne, Michel de, 15, 21
Mother Idea, 8, 20–21, 25, 30, 39–42, 62–63,
82, 84

Napoleon, 52–53

papal bulls, 17, 21, 23, 68
papal encyclicals, 22, 82–83
Paris convents, 8, 12–13, 55
Pascal, Blaise, 107
pensionnat, 28, 36, 58, 60, 68, 102
popes: Gregory I, 120; Leo XIII, 58, 79, 82–83,
87; Paul III, 17–18, 21, 23, 84; Paul V,
17, 23, 56, 68, 145; Pius IX, 83; Pius XI,
82–84, 87
Primitive Ursulines, 24
privilège du roi, 6, 11–13, 24, 94

Rabelais, François, 15, 21
Ratio studiorum, 9, 26–27, 90

Redefining Female Religious Life (Lux-Sterritt), 3, 6, 22–25

Règle de Nostre Père Saint Augustin. See rule of Saint Augustine

Règlemens pour les religieuses de Saincte Ursule de la congrégation de Paris, 14

Regola della Compagnia di S. Orsola, 18–19

reprintings: *Règlemens* of 1705, 12, 56, 94; *Règlements* of 1860, 56

Richelet, César-Pierre, 122–23

Rogers, Rebecca, 52, 66, 146

Roman Catechism, 46, 48, 101, 112

Roman Union of the Order of Saint Ursuline, 79–81

rule of Saint Augustine, 11, 23–24

sacraments, preparation for: Confirmation, 38, 46, 114–15, 119, 155, 159; Eucharist, 37–39, 117–19; First Communion, 36, 38, 70, 98, 112, 116–22, 142–46, 155, 159; general confession, 25, 38, 46, 98, 112–15, 117–20, 146, 154–55, 158–59, 163; Penance, 25, 113, 118–19, 146

St. Cyr, 15–16

St. Jean Martin, Mother Marie de, ix, 6–7, 9–10, 12–13, 22, 26–27, 55–56, 79–91

St. John's College, Annapolis, MD, 84

Saint-Jure, Jean Baptiste, 120

Saint Ursula, 4, 16

Sainte-Beuve, Mme de, 22, 27

Sévigné, Mme de, 9, 66

Spiritual Exercises (Ignatius of Loyola), 9

University of Notre Dame, 84

Ursuline Academy, New Orleans, ix, 1–5, 91

Ursuline Method of Education (St. Jean Martin), 6–7, 10, 79–91

Ursulines: in New Orleans, 3, 5, 12, 17, 24, 91; in Quebec, 1–2, 17, 23, 86–87; in Rouen, 1, 5, 17; in St. Louis, MO, ix; in Toulouse, 13, 24; in Trois Rivières, 86

Vatican II, 7, 32, 91

Voices from an Early American Convent (Clark), 3

CPSIA information can be obtained
at www.ICGtesting.com
Printed in the USA
LVHW100843031222
734345LV00005B/486